Learning Through Literature

Mary Jane Butner
Jane Ann Peterson
Janice Marks Sieplinga

Illustrated by Janice Marks Sieplinga

Scott, Foresman and Company
Glenview, Illinois   London

Dedication

To our children for their patience
Andrew, Nicholas, and Matthew Butner
Glenn, Greg, and Paul Peterson
Jonathan Sieplinga

To our husbands for their support
John Butner
Dale Peterson
Larry Sieplinga

To our parents for their encouragement
John and Mary Shields
Ryan and Gail Zuidema
Ed and Evelyn Marks

 **Good Year Books**

are available for preschool through grade 8 and for every basic curriculum subject plus many enrichment areas. For more Good Year Books, contact your local bookseller or educational dealer. For a complete catalog with information about other Good Year Books, please write:

Good Year Books
Scott, Foresman and Company
1900 East Lake Avenue
Glenview, Illinois 60025

1 2 3 4 5 6 MCG 95 94 93 92 91 90

ISBN 0-673-46076-2

Contents

Preface

All the media attention on the problem of illiteracy in America has made parents and educators eager to find ways to instill a love of books in young children. That is why **Learning Through Literature** was written. The following pages are intended to provide preschool, kindergarten, and primary teachers with the means to help children discover the value and enjoyment of books.

Early exposure to literature is critically important to developing reading ability. Young children need to have books read to them regularly—at school as well as at home. Listening to stories helps children broaden their experiences and vocabulary.

By also providing stimulating activities that complement the stories, teachers can heighten children's enjoyment of books. **Learning Through Literature** offers a wide range of activities, all of which stimulate creative expression and thinking and give children a variety of sensory and manipulative experiences. The range of these activities is so wide, in fact, that **Learning Through Literature** will meet the needs of children who differ greatly in age, ability, and learning style.

In addition to the classroom teacher, librarians, child care givers, and substitute teachers can make good use of these activities. Librarians can incorporate many of the activities into story hour and enrichment programs. Caregivers in day care centers and latchkey programs can adapt the ideas to a variety of age groups. And substitute teachers, when in need of an emergency resource, will appreciate the easily reproduced worksheets.

Acknowledgments

We would like to thank our teacher colleagues who have inspired us over the years and who have shared and traded ideas with us.
In addition, we would like to thank those school administrators we have worked for who gave us free rein to create our own curriculum.

We would especially like to acknowledge and thank the children we have taught. Their enthusiastic response to our Storybook Friends unit encouraged us to put our ideas into a book.

How to Use This Book

For every book presented in the following pages, **_Learning Through Literature_** provides a variety of activities under these headings:

Introductory Activities

This section includes suggestions for stimulating language development, setting the scene, introducing characters and ideas, and having the children make predictions about the story. Very often we use an item in the "Surprise Box" to initiate discussion. To make a "Surprise Box," cover a shoe box with contact paper and cut a hole in one end so that children can feel—but not see— an item inside.

Art Activities

The art activities are significant because they provide the children with concrete reminders to use as aids at home in retelling the stories to their parents. They also provide the children with an opportunity to explore various art media. Many of the art ideas invite a creative response to the story; others, accompanied by reproducible worksheets, are designed to strengthen specific skills. Any activity throughout the book that has an accompanying reproducible worksheet has an asterisk [*] to indicate that fact.

Language Development

In addition to providing the teacher with ideas for stimulating creative thinking, strengthening expressive and receptive language skills, and sharpening reading readiness skills, this section contains writing activities, vocabulary words, and questions aimed at developing higher-level thinking skills. "Words to Grow By" includes words from the story that may not be part of the children's speaking/listening vocabulary. In cases where the vocabulary in a story is minimal, we have included words that the teacher and students might use in a discussion of a story.

Fine and Gross Motor Development

Young children need many opportunities to exercise and refine their small and large muscles. These activities not only provide such opportunities but also heighten the children's enjoyment of the story.

Fingerplays and Songs

Many concepts are more easily taught and better remembered through the repetition, rhythm, and patterns in fingerplays and songs. Each story has at least one original fingerplay and song. Songs are set to familiar tunes.

Cooking and Science

These two sections provide additional opportunities for children to observe, discuss, explore, and create.

Math

The activities in this section will help children develop math concepts: graphs, seriation, comparisons, grouping, counting, measuring.

Extended Experiences and Related Books

The activities in these sections will help the teacher who wants to continue or expand each lesson, carrying over to another day.

A Few Suggestions

Learning Through Literature is not a formal curriculum. Rather, it is a resource for an informal learning approach. You choose the activities that are best suited to your students' needs, interests, and abilities.

Preschool and kindergarten teachers can choose activities from each section and have a complete lesson plan for one day. They may even find enough ideas to plan several days of activities around a particular theme or storybook character. How about a Clifford, Curious George, or Frances week? Or have a dental health, nutrition, or dinosaur week!

Primary teachers may choose to use the vocabulary words, questions, story maps, and story frames as enrichment activities. They can prepare the directions for many of the other activities for use in a learning center. For example, children enjoy practicing their comprehension skills by following the directions for an art activity.

The "Language Development" section often has riddles. Although the riddles are designed as a receptive language activity for very young children, primary children can copy the riddles for printing practice and draw pictures of the answers as a comprehension activity. Because young children need a great deal of modeling in order to realize their potential as writers, **Learning Through Literature** offers the "Structured Story Starter (SSS)." Besides helping children develop writing skills, this device makes them more aware of patterns, structure, style, and an author's viewpoint in literature.

To use the Structured Story Starter, write the SSS outline on the chalkboard and have the children create a story together. Reproduce this story in book form and give each child a copy. The children can then illustrate each page and take turns reading parts of the story out loud. On another day, try giving each child a copy of the SSS and ask them to develop their own stories. On the following pages you'll find Structured Story Starters for *Clifford the Small Red Puppy, Curious George,* and *Stone Soup.*

Although many of the activities were designed with younger children in mind, they appeal to early elementary children too. Primary teachers can incorporate the motor activities into their gym period, or the songs and art into music and art periods.

These are just a few suggestions for using this book. You will undoubtedly have many more ideas of your own. Remember that *you,* the teacher, are the most important element in breathing life into the storybook characters. Your enthusiasm is the key ingredient in helping children discover the joy and excitement of reading.

Celebrate books!

ANIMALS

Frederick
Frederick

Clifford Hand Puppet
Clifford

Hatching Baby Dinosaurs
The Day of the Dinosaur

Corduroy, Don Freeman
A Pocket for Corduroy, Don Freeman
The Day of the Dinosaur, Stan and Jan Berenstain
Clifford the Small Red Puppy, Norman Bridwell
Make Way for Ducklings, Robert McCloskey
Frederick, Leo Lionni
Caps for Sale, Esphyr Slobodkina
Curious George, H. A. Rey

BEARS

Corduroy, Don Freeman, The Viking Press, 1968.
Who wants to buy a little toy bear, even though there's a button missing on his overalls? Lisa does!

A Pocket for Corduroy, Don Freeman, The Viking Press, 1978.
Corduroy discovers pockets and realizes he doesn't have one. He explores a laundromat while searching for a pocket.

Introductory Activities

Surprise Box   Put a button, toy bear, or piece of corduroy material inside the surprise box.

Group Discussion   Talk about whether anyone is wearing corduroy.

Art Activities

*Bear Pattern and Overall Pattern   Use the patterns to represent Corduroy in many different ways:

*Best Overall Bear   Have the children cut the bear out of brown construction paper. They can draw facial features and paste on overalls made of green construction paper or real corduroy. After reading _A Pocket for Corduroy,_ let the children add a purple pocket and a small slip of paper that says "Corduroy."

*Indicates activity that has an accompanying reproducible worksheet.

*Sudsy Bear
Have the children spread brown soap paint inside the bear shape. While the soap is still wet, add facial features and overalls made of green corrugated paper—they will stick to the soap paint. (Make soap paint by mixing 2 cups of powdered detergent with lukewarm water, adding the water gradually and mixing to the consistency of whipped cream.)

*Yummy Bear
Let the children use instant chocolate pudding to fill in the bear shape.

Fingerpainting
Let the children swirl different fingerpaint colors around on the bear pattern—imitating clothes going around in a dryer.

*Movable Bear
Using the Movable Bear pattern, make a bear of construction paper. Attach the bear's arms and legs with brass fasteners.

Cloth and Button Collage
Encourage the children to make a collage using buttons and different kinds of cloth—including corduroy, of course! They can make the collage on a large tagboard bear.

Language Development

Words to Grow By

Corduroy	*A Pocket for Corduroy*	
department	laundry	swirling colors
escalator	patiently	steep mountainside
palace	precious	drowsy
night watchman	dampness	señorita
furniture	cave	rascal
customers	reluctant	affectionate
apartment	beret	
enormous	dizzy	
comfortable	sketch pad	

---

*Indicates activity that has an accompanying reproducible worksheet.

From *Learning Through Literature*, published by Scott, Foresman and Company.
Copyright © 1991 Mary Jane Butner, Jane Ann Peterson, and Janice Marks Sieplinga.

Something to Think About

Corduroy

Where did Corduroy live?

Why didn't Lisa's mother want to buy Corduroy?

How was the furniture department similar to a house? How was it different?

Is it important what your friends look like?

Why don't people want to buy things that are not perfect or are not packaged?

Be a salesman—talk someone into buying a bear with a missing button.

A Pocket for Corduroy

Where were Lisa and her mother going?

Explain what a laundromat is.

Pretend that you are going to the laundromat. What will you need? What will you do when you get there?

Some people do laundry at home. Tell why it would be easier than going to a laundromat. What advantages might there be in going to the laundromat?

Did Corduroy do something that he should not have done? Why is wandering off _not_ a good idea?

Teddy Bear Show and Tell

Give awards to _all_ bears who come for "Show and Tell" — biggest, smallest, softest, most realistic, etc.

Dramatic Play

Set up a "laundry" in the housekeeping center where children can wash, hang up, and fold clothing. Provide a clothesline, clothespins, and empty detergent boxes and bottles.

Lost in a Department Store

Ask the children how they would feel and what they would do if they became separated from their parents while shopping at a large store. Consider using the situation as a creative dramatics activity or as a creative writing exercise. Record the ideas of the younger children.

---

*Indicates activity that has an accompanying reproducible worksheet._

| **The Department Store** | Make a "department store" on posterboard. Divide the board into toy, clothing, and furniture departments. Provide pictures of items that fit into these categories (you can draw the pictures or cut them out of old magazines and catalogs). Have the children identify the items and place them in the correct departments. |

| **The Toy Department** | Place four to six toys in front of the children. Select one child to be the "clerk." The clerk asks three children to come to the toy department, and each child buys a toy. The three then return to their seats, hiding their toys from the clerk. The clerk must then identify each child and the toy she bought. |

| ***Story Frame** | A story frame helps children recall details and identify main ideas in a story. |

Fine and Gross Motor Skills

| **Button Sorting and Stringing** | Start a button collection, and have the children sort them—by size, color, or shape. Provide thin laces for stringing buttons. |

| ***Button Hunt** | The children must use their eyes to find the 20 buttons hidden in the picture. |

| ***Toy Shadow Match** | Have the children draw lines to match each toy with its shadow. |

| **Textures** | Collect duplicate sets of swatches of many different fabrics, including corduroy. Put one set in a "feelie bag." Have a child look at and feel a piece of fabric from the other set and then see if she can find its match in the bag. |

*Indicates activity that has an accompanying reproducible worksheet.

Clothesline   Let the children hang laundry on a clothesline, using both straight and clip clothespins.

Button Walk   This game is best played with three to five children. The leader hides a button in one hand and extends both closed fists to the children, who must guess which hand is holding the button. The children who guess correctly take a step forward. The winner of the game is the first child to reach the finish line.

Bear Walk   Have the children walk like real bears. A bear moves his right front paw, left back paw, left front, and finally right back paw—and then repeats the sequence. Have the children practice the bear walk, and then have a bear-walk relay race.

Who's Sitting On the Button?   This game requires that the children use both their listening and thinking skills. Have them start by sitting in a circle. Select one child to close his eyes. Silently give another child a button to sit on. The first child then walks around the circle. When he is far from the button, the children clap softly; when he nears the person sitting on the button, the children clap loudly until he discovers who has the button. Continue the game until every child has had a turn being "it."

Button Search   Hide a quantity of buttons and let the children try to find them.

Pass the Teddy   Give the children a teddy bear to pass around while you play some music. When the music stops, the child holding the bear is "out." Continue the game until just one child is left. With very young children, modify the game by not eliminating anyone; just have them keep passing the teddy bear for the fun of it.

Indicates activity that has an accompanying reproducible worksheet.

Fingerplays and Songs _____

Going On A Button Hunt
by Mary Jane Butner, Jane Peterson, Janice Marks Sieplinga

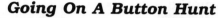

(Rhythmically chant each line with the children repeating after you.)

Corduroy needs a button.
Let's help him find one.
All right, let's go!

Oh look, we're on a toy shelf.
Can't go over it.
Can't go through it.
Let's climb down it.
All right, let's go!

(Pretend to climb down.)

Oh look, we're on the first floor.
Look at all the toys here.
I see a pogo stick.
Can't go over it.
Can't go under it.
Better jump on it.
All right, let's go!
Boing, boing, boing!

(Pretend to jump on pogo stick.)

Let's go up the escalator.

(Slowly rise from a squatting to a standing position.)

Oh look, we're on the second floor.
Look at all the clothes here.
I see a clothes rack.
Can't go over it.
Can't go under it.
Let's go through it.
All right, let's go!
Swish, swish, swish!

(Pretend to move clothes away with arms and hands.)

---

*Indicates activity that has an accompanying reproducible worksheet.

Let's go up the escalator.

Oh look, we're on the third floor.
Look at all the dishes here.
Can't go near them.
Must not touch them.
Better go away from them.
All right, tiptoe!

(Tiptoe.)

Let's go up the escalator.

Oh look, we're on the fourth floor.
Look at all the sporting goods. I see a big tent.
Can't go over it.
Can't go around it.
Let's crawl through it.
All right, let's go!

(Pretend to crawl through tent.)

Let's go up the escalator.

Oh look, we're on the fifth floor.
Look at all the furniture.
I see a big bed.
Can't go under it.
Can't go around it.
Let's climb on it.
All right, let's go!

(Pretend to climb up on bed and look for button.)

Oh look!
I found my button.
Help me pull it!

(Pretend to pull button and then crash to the floor.)

---

*Indicates activity that has an accompanying reproducible worksheet.

Corduroy, Corduroy
by Mary Jane Butner, Jane Peterson, Janice Marks Sieplinga

Corduroy, Corduroy, jump up and down.
Corduroy, Corduroy, hop around.
Corduroy, Corduroy, go up on your toes.
Corduroy, Corduroy, touch your nose.
Corduroy, Corduroy, wave your hand.
Corduroy, Corduroy, wink if you can.
Corduroy, Corduroy, bend down low.
Corduroy, Corduroy, sit just so.

Teddy Wore His Overalls
(Tune: "Mary Had a Little Lamb")

Teddy wore his overalls, overalls, overalls.
Teddy wore his overalls to school today.

Before "Corduroy" day, send a note home asking that the children wear something green, something made of corduroy, or overalls. Sing the song several times, substituting the names of the children and their colors and clothes.

Cooking _____

Beary Honey Sandwiches   Give the children bear cookie cutters and let them cut bear shapes out of bread. They can then spread honey or honey butter on the bear cutouts.

Science _____

Animal Homes   Discuss different kinds of animal homes—nests, hills, dens, caves, dams, barns, etc. Draw pictures of different animals and their homes (or cut out pictures from magazines) so that the children can play a matching game.

Indicates activity that has an accompanying reproducible worksheet.

Animal Prints   If possible, take a field trip into the woods and search for animal footprints. You can even make plaster castings of prints for study back in the classroom.

Math

Count Buttons   Give children different quantities of buttons to count.

*Buttons 'n Sweaters   Use the patterns to make several sweaters. Put a number and a corresponding quantity of buttonholes on each one. Have the children place the correct number of bingo markers or real buttons on each sweater.

Extended Experiences

Visit a Department Store   Take the children on a field trip to a department store. Ride the escalator. Visit the toy and furniture departments.

Visit a Laundromat   Take the children on a field trip to a laundromat. If time allows, actually wash and dry some dress-up clothes and dolly clothes.

Related Books

Beady Bear, Don Freeman, The Viking Press, 1954 (reprint Puffin Books, 1979).
  A story in rhyme about a wind-up bear and his friend Thayer.

Bearymore, Don Freeman, The Viking Press, 1976.
  A circus bear looks for a new act.

*Indicates activity that has an accompanying reproducible worksheet.

From _Learning Through Literature_, published by Scott, Foresman and Company.
Copyright © 1991 Mary Jane Butner, Jane Ann Peterson, and Janice Marks Sieplinga.

Bear Pattern

Overall Pattern

Movable Bear

Movable Bear

arms and legs

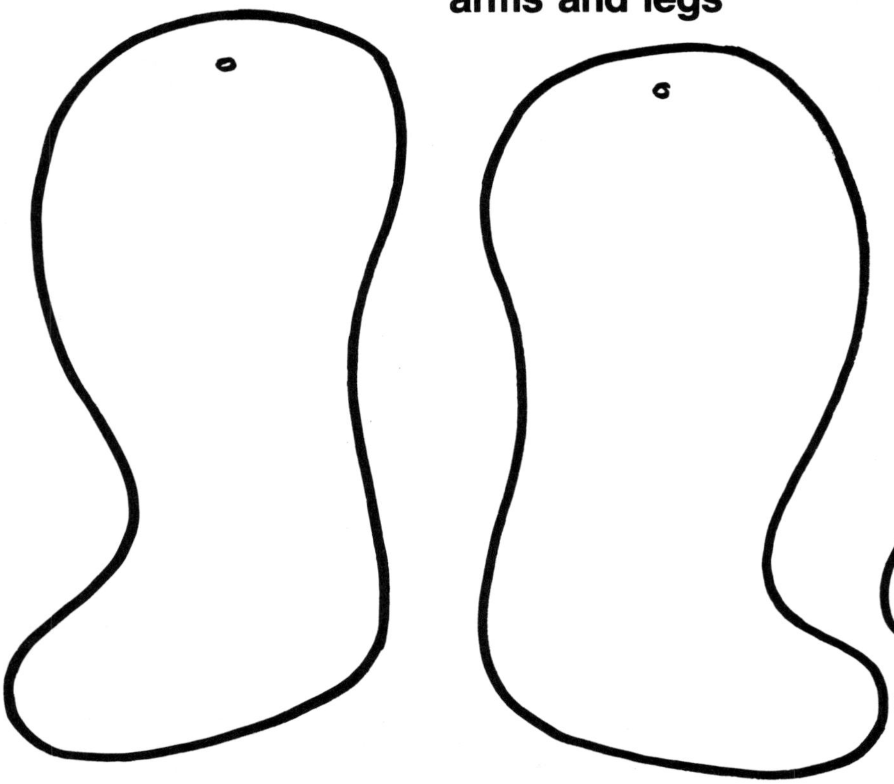

need 2

Buttons 'n Sweaters

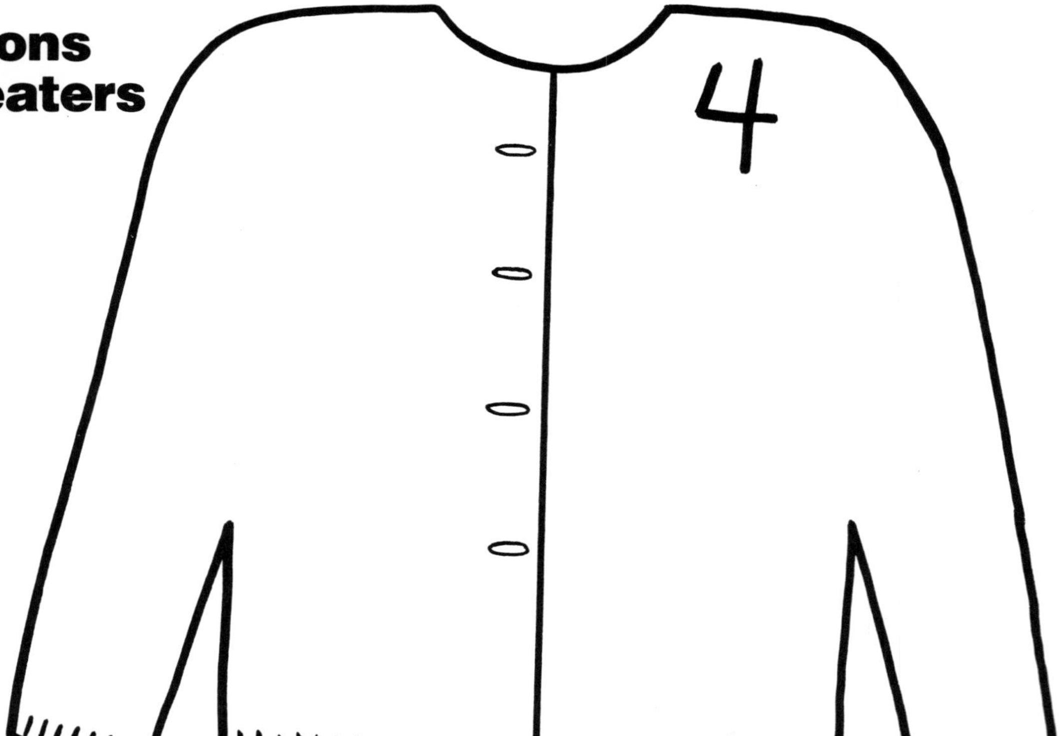

4

Name _____

Story Frame: *Corduroy*

Corduroy is a bear who wants _____

_____

Lisa's mother will not buy him because _____

_____

Corduroy decides to _____

_____

So he goes _____

_____

The night watchman _____

_____

The next day, Lisa _____

_____

At the end of the story, _____

_____

Button Hunt

Name _____

Toy Shadow Match

From *Learning Through Literature*, published by Scott, Foresman and Company.
Copyright © 1991 Mary Jane Butner, Jane Ann Peterson, and Janice Marks Sieplinga.

DINOSAURS

The Day of the Dinosaur, Stan and Jan Berenstain, Random House, 1987.
   The Berenstains have put their humorous rhyming style to good use, effectively introducing factual information about dinosaurs.

Introductory Activity

Surprise Box   Put a toy dinosaur, a bone, or a fossil inside the surprise box. By placing a plastic egg inside the box, you may spark a discussion of all the animals children can think of that hatch from eggs (including dinosaurs!).

Art Activities

*Apatosaurus   Reproduce the pattern, using any color of construction paper. The children cut out the body, head, and tail, and then attach the parts with paper fasteners.

*Hatching Baby Dinosaurs

Reproduce the egg pattern and let the children use their imaginations to decorate dinosaur eggs. They then cut the eggs out and cut a jagged line from dot to dot "to crack the egg open." Each child then chooses a baby dinosaur and attaches it to the egg with a paper fastener.

Create a Dinosaur   Have the children design and name new dinosaurs.

---

*Indicates activity that has an accompanying reproducible worksheet.

*Dino-myte Patterns

Use an opaque projector to enlarge the dinosaur patterns—the bigger the better! Let the children use their imaginations to paint the creatures the way they think dinosaurs might have looked. Allow them to use paintbrushes or fingerpaints or even sponges to dab on their designs.

*Shadow Dinosaurs

Let each child choose a "Dino-myte Pattern" and cut out two—one from a sheet of colored paper, the other from a sheet of black paper. After drawing a background of plants and trees, the child then pastes the pair of dinosaurs so that the black shape creates a "shadow" for the colored one.

*Other Dino-myte Ideas

Let the children use the "Dino-myte Patterns" to make stick puppets or mobiles, murals or collages. Encourage the children to design placemats from enlarged patterns; laminate the placemats and allow the children to use them at snack time. You can also use the patterns to make puzzles, matching activities, and flannelboard cutouts.

Leaf Dinosaurs

Challenge the children to create dinosaurs from the leaves of trees that grow in your area. Let them use whole leaves, parts of leaves, and various leaf combinations to create their dinosaurs.

Language Development

Words to Grow By

roamed	reckless	prehistoric
skeletons	nostrils	rhino-tusks
scientists	carnivore	beneath
fossils	splendid	flightless
fierce	back-sail	gigantic
jaws	wingspan	extinct
ferocity	lofty	exist
armored	crest	disaster
armored-plated	creatures	

Indicates activity that has an accompanying reproducible worksheet.

From *Learning Through Literature*, published by Scott, Foresman and Company.
Copyright © 1991 Mary Jane Butner, Jane Ann Peterson, and Janice Marks Sieplinga.

The Day of the Dinosaur provides a guide to help the children (and teacher) pronounce the names of the dinosaurs correctly.

Something to Think About

Do dinosaurs live today?
Has anyone ever seen a living dinosaur?
How do scientists know that dinosaurs really existed?
If an Apatosaurus (or Triceratops, Tyrannosaurus, etc.) came to your house, what would you feed it?
List some of the plant-eating dinosaurs, some meat-eating dinosaurs.
How was Pteranodon like a bird? How was it different?
Why do you think dinosaurs became extinct?
Which dinosaur would you most like to meet (or not meet!)? Explain your reasons.

My Pet Dinosaur

Older children can write their own dinosaur stories. Younger children can dictate their ideas to an adult.

My Book of Dinosaurs

Have the children draw and color pictures of dinosaurs— one per page—and then print the name of each dinosaur and one important fact about it.

Dinosaur Riddles

Have pictures of a wide variety of dinosaurs. You can often find packs of dinosaur cards at museum shops. Display the pictures and ask the children to name or point to the dinosaur that matches each description.
    He had a sail on his back. (Dimetrodon)
    He had bony spikes on his thumbs. (Iguanodon)
    He had bony plates on his back. (Stegosaurus)
    He was the first true bird. (Archaeopteryx)

Alphabetical Dinosaurs

Challenge the children to think of a dinosaur name for every letter of the alphabet. Even very young children know enough about beginning sounds that they may surprise you on this activity.

Indicates activity that has an accompanying reproducible worksheet.

From *Learning Through Literature*, published by Scott, Foresman and Company.
Copyright © 1991 Mary Jane Butner, Jane Ann Peterson, and Janice Marks Sieplinga.

*Apatosaurus Word Game

See how many words the children can make from the letters in "Apatosaurus." This word game gives older children an opportunity to practice their spelling, phonics, and printing skills.

Fine and Gross Motor Skills _____

*What Did Dinosaurs Eat?

Before handing out this worksheet, you may want to discuss herbivores (plant-eaters) and carnivores (meat-eaters). Point out that carnivores have sharp pointy teeth for tearing meat while herbivores have flat-edged teeth for grinding.

*Stegosaurus Maze

Reproduce this maze to help the children develop fine motor control, tracking, and decision-making skills.

*Dinosaur Match

Make copies of this matching activity to help the children develop visual discrimination skills.

Puzzles

Many dinosaur puzzles are available through school supply catalogs, or you can make your own simple jigsaw puzzles out of posterboard. Cut each picture into three or four pieces, and draw an outline on another piece of posterboard as a guide for doing the puzzle.

*Funny Dinosaurs

Make felt cutouts from the "Dino-myte Patterns." Cut each dinosaur in half. Then let the children create new "funny dinosaurs" by combining various heads and bodies. As an alternate activity, you can scramble all the pieces and challenge the children to put each dinosaur back together correctly.

---

*Indicates activity that has an accompanying reproducible worksheet.

*Shadow Dinosaurs Game

Cut out and laminate two of each pattern from the "Dino-myte Patterns," using colored paper for one and black paper for the other. Have the children match each dinosaur with its shadow.

Play Dough

Provide modeling dough so that the children can mold three-dimensional dinosaurs. You might also bring in some dinosaur cookie cutters (available through catalogs or in museum gift shops) for the children to use.

Dinosaur Stomp

Encourage the children to move like dinosaurs. Some should walk on all fours while others are upright. Some should move as they imagine big heavy dinosaurs would while others should move like small light ones. The children can reach up "to eat the leaves off trees"; they can snarl and chase each other; fly like pteranodons, etc.

Tyrannosaurus Tag

Spread carpet squares around the room or gym for all but one child; that child is designated Tyrannosaurus Rex. At a signal, all the children run to new squares while Tyrannosaurus tries to catch one off a square. A child who gets caught becomes the new Tyrannosaurus and the old Tyrannosaurus becomes a prey. As a variation, you can allow each Tyrannosaurus to remain a Tyrannosaurus until the whole class has been caught.

Dinosaur Bones

Make bones from white posterboard and put them on the floor. The children will develop eye-foot coordination as they walk around the bones, step or jump over them.

---

*Indicates activity that has an accompanying reproducible worksheet.

Tyrannosaurus Rex's Cave

This is an outdoor game. One child is Tyrannosaurus Rex, another is Mother Brontosaurus, and the rest are Baby Brontosaurs. Designate one area as the Tyrannosaurus's cave and another area as Mother Brontosaurus's home. The babies go to their mother and say, "Mother, Mother, may we go out to play?" She responds, "Yes, but stay away from Tyrannosaurus's cave." The babies then creep close to the cave. When Mother Brontosaurus calls out, "Children come home," Tyrannosaurus chases them. Any babies that get caught become Tyrannosaurs and help with the chase. The game is over when only one Brontosaurus is left.

Fingerplays and Songs _____

Dinosaur Race
by Mary Jane Butner and Jane Peterson

Triceratops with his three-horned face,
Apatosaurus who stayed in one place,
Pteranodon who soared with grace,
Saw Tyrannosaurus—and boy did they race!

Distinctly Extinct
by Mary Jane Butner and Jane Peterson

Five ancient dinosaurs, walking down the trail.
Diplodocus said, "Don't step on my tail."
Compsognathus said, "I am the smallest."
Ultrasaurus said, "I am the tallest."
Deinonychus said, "I have sharp claws."
Tyrannosaurus said, "Watch out for my jaws!"

Five ancient dinosaurs—each one quite distinct.
But, I'm sad to say, they all are now extinct.

*Indicates activity that has an accompanying reproducible worksheet.

Dinosaurs
by Mary Jane Butner
(Tune: "The Bear Went Over the Mountain")

Stegosaurus had bony plates, Stegosaurus had bony plates,
Stegosaurus had bony plates all along his back.

Triceratops had three horns, Triceratops had three horns,
Triceratops had three horns; he wore them on his face.

Pteranodon could fly, Pteranodon could fly,
Pteranodon could fly; he had skin-covered wings.

Tyrannosaurus had sharp teeth, Tyrannosaurus had sharp teeth,
Tyrannosaurus had sharp teeth; he'd eat you if he could!

Learn About Dinosaurs
by Jane Peterson
(Tune: "Love and Marriage")

Apatosaurus, Tyrannosaurus,
These are dinosaurs that lived before us.
I'm glad I've never met one.
'Cause if I did I'd never pet one.

Triceratops with his three horns—
He looks pretty scary.
Pteranodon flying through the air—
Of him you'd best be wary!

Allosaurus, Stegosaurus,
All are dinosaurs that lived before us.
See them at the museum.
See the fossils there.
Which you can compare.
Learn about them—WHERE?
At the museum!

*Indicates activity that has an accompanying reproducible worksheet.

Dinosaur Guessing Game

by Mary Jane Butner

(Tune: "Frère Jacques." Before playing this singing game, give each child a stick puppet of a Stegosaurus, Pteranodon, Triceratops, Tyrannosaurus, or Dimetrodon. During the song, the children hold up the correct puppet in response to the questions.)

TEACHER:
Who has bony plates?
Who has bony plates?

STUDENTS:
Here I am.
Here I am.
I'm a Stegosaurus. I have bony plates.
Here I am. Here I am.

TEACHER:
Who has leather wings?
Who has leather wings?

STUDENTS:
Here I am.
Here I am.
I'm a Pteranodon. I have leather wings.
Here I am. Here I am.

TEACHER:
Who has three horns?
Who has three horns?

STUDENTS:
Here I am.
Here I am.
I'm a Triceratops. I have three horns.
Here I am. Here I am.

TEACHER:
Who has sharp teeth?
Who has sharp teeth?

*Indicates activity that has an accompanying reproducible worksheet.

STUDENTS:
Here I am.
Here I am.
I'm a Tyrannosaurus. I have sharp teeth.
Here I am. Here I am.

TEACHER:
Who has a back-sail?
Who has a back-sail?

STUDENTS:
Here I am.
Here I am.
I'm a Dimetrodon. I have a back-sail.
Here I am. Here I am.

Who likes Dinosaurs?

by Mary Jane Butner
(Tune: "Short Shorts." If you're not familiar with this song from the
50s, ask an "elderly" colleague to sing it for you.)

Who likes dinosaurs?
We like dinosaurs.
We like Stegosaurs.
And we like Brontosaurs.
Dimetrodon, Triceratops,
Pteranodon, and Eryops—
We like dinosaurs—oh yeah!

Cooking _____

**Dinosaur
Sandwiches**

Give the children dinosaur cookie cutters, and let them cut
out bread, cheese, and bologna for sandwiches. Or let them
use the cookie cutters to make shapes out of bread and
then spread peanut butter or cream cheese on the bread.
They can even give their dinosaurs eyes by adding raisins.

Jiggly Dinosaurs

Let the children use dinosaur cookie cutters to cut shapes
in finger gelatin.

Indicates activity that has an accompanying reproducible worksheet.

Science

Fossils

Display fossils. If you can't borrow them from a science teacher, you can buy them at many rock exhibitions and at museum shops.

Fossil Footprints

Press small amounts of clay or play dough into the bottom of several margarine tub lids. Make footprints of several dinosaur models by pressing their feet in the clay. Put the footprints and models on the science table and see if the children can match each dinosaur with its footprint.

Who Comes From An Egg?

Challenge the children to name as many animals as they can think of that hatch out of eggs.

Plant-Eater or Meat-Eater?

Plant Eaters ♥	Meat Eaters ●
Apatosaurus	

Make a two-column chart with the headings "Plant-Eater" and "Meat-Eater." Have the children lay dinosaur models or pictures on the chart in the appropriate columns. If they are unsure about where to place a dinosaur, help them to deduce the answer by telling them whether the dinosaur had sharp teeth or flat teeth.

Math

Dinosaur Match-Ups

Buy some rubber stamps of various dinosaurs (available in catalogs, museum shops, and toy stores). Make 10 dinosaur eggs out of posterboard. Put a number on one end of each egg and stamp a corresponding number of dinosaurs on the other end. Then cut the eggs in half, making a different jagged line for each. Have the children count the dinosaurs and match each with its number.

Indicates activity that has an accompanying reproducible worksheet.

Dinosaur Graph   If you do the "Hatching Baby Dinosaurs" activity (Art
                       Activities), make a graph with the heading "Which
                       dinosaur did you choose?" The children can mark their
                       choices in the columns and then count the responses to
                       find the most-chosen and least-chosen dinosaurs.

Extended Experience ——————————————————

Field Trip   If you are close to a museum that has a dinosaur display,
                       take a field trip.

Related Books ——————————————————

Bruno Brontosaurus, Nicole Rubel, Avon Books, 1983.
   Bruno is different from his siblings: he likes to swim while they like
   to fight; he has a craving for plants while they eat meat. Is it
   possible that he is the victim of a mix-up?

Danny and the Dinosaur, Syd Hoff, Harper & Row, 1958.
   Wouldn't it be fun to have a dinosaur for a pet?

Dinosaurs, A Lost World, Keith Mosely and Robert Cremins, G. P.
Putnam's Sons, 1984.
   Children enjoy looking at this beautifully designed and executed pop-
   up book.

Patrick's Dinosaurs, Carol Carrick, Clarion Books, Ticknor & Fields (a
Houghton-Mifflin Company), 1983.
   Patrick imagines that he is being threatened by the dinosaurs that
   his brother has described to him. Patrick's fears evaporate when he
   learns that dinosaurs are extinct.

The following are factual books about dinosaurs:

Dinosaurs, Kathleen N. Daly, Golden Press, Western Publishing
Company, 1977.
Dinosaurs, Peter Zallinger, Random House, 1977.
A New True Book of Dinosaurs, Mary Lou Clark, Childrens Press,
1955, 1981.
Prehistoric Animals, Peter Zallinger, Random House, 1978.

Indicates activity that has an accompanying reproducible worksheet.

Apatosaurus
(formerly called Brontosaurus)

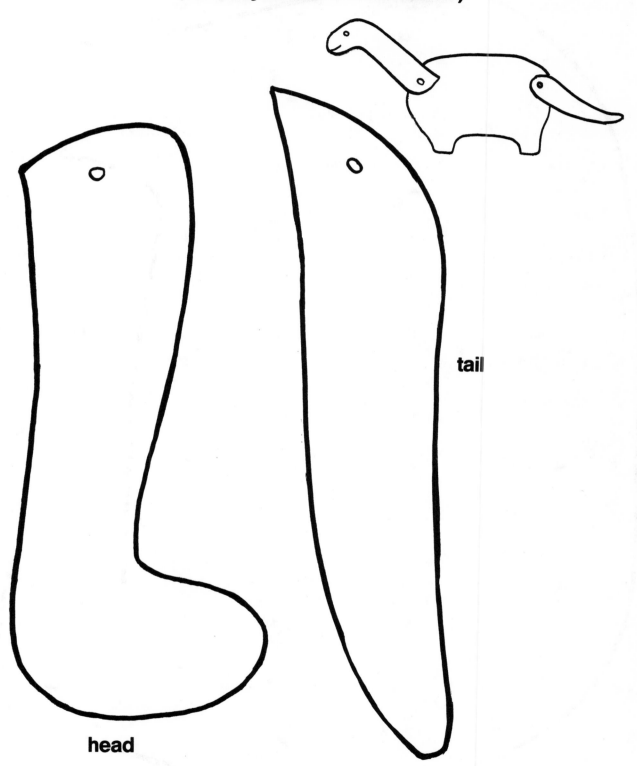

tail

head

Apatosaurus

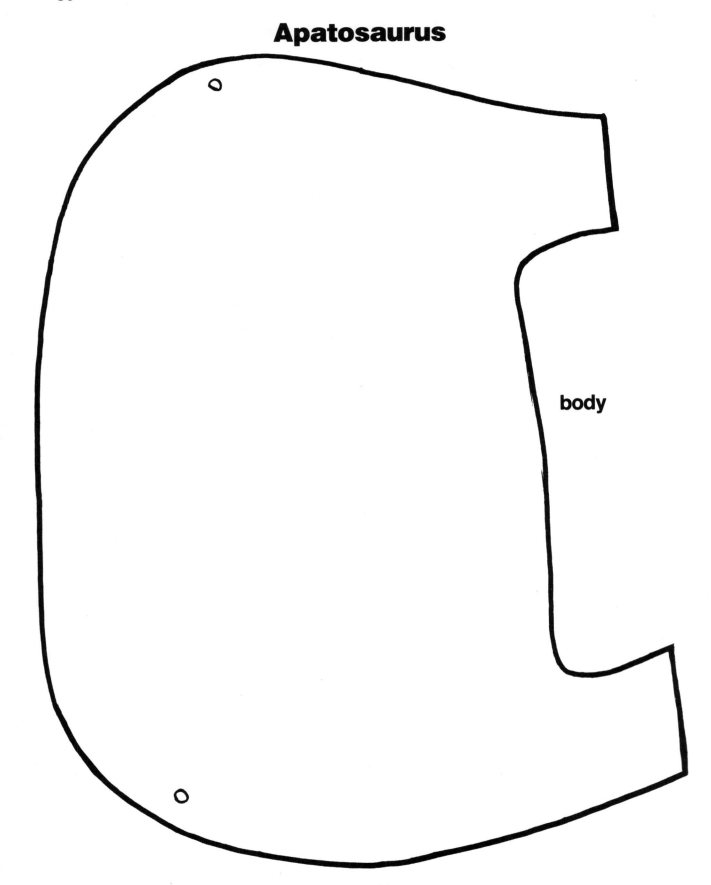

body

Hatching Baby Dinosaurs

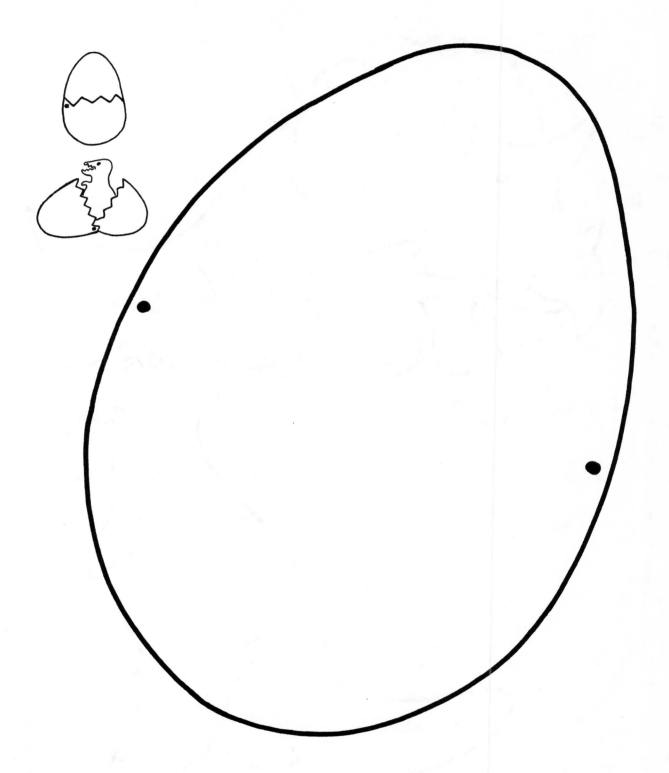

Hatching Baby Dinosaurs

Dino-myte Patterns

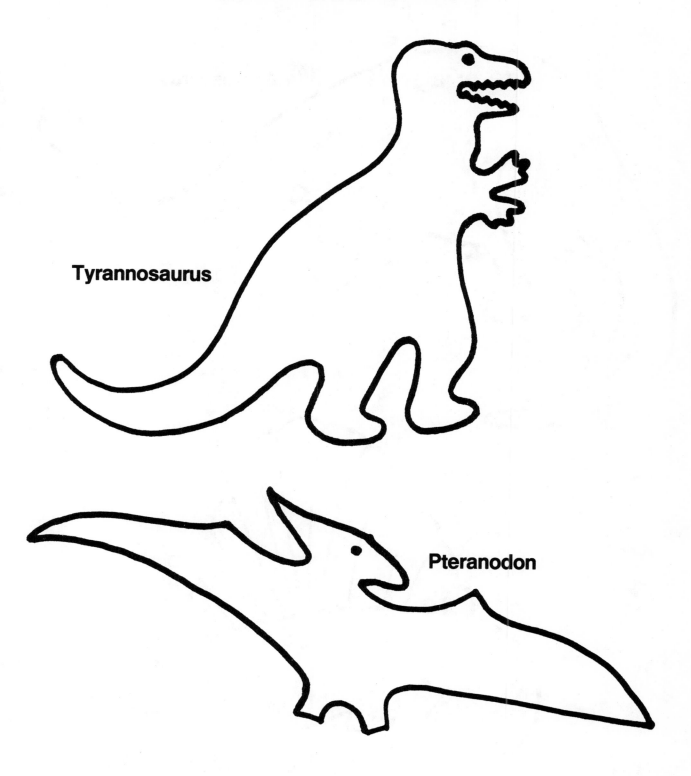

Tyrannosaurus

Pteranodon

Dino-myte Patterns

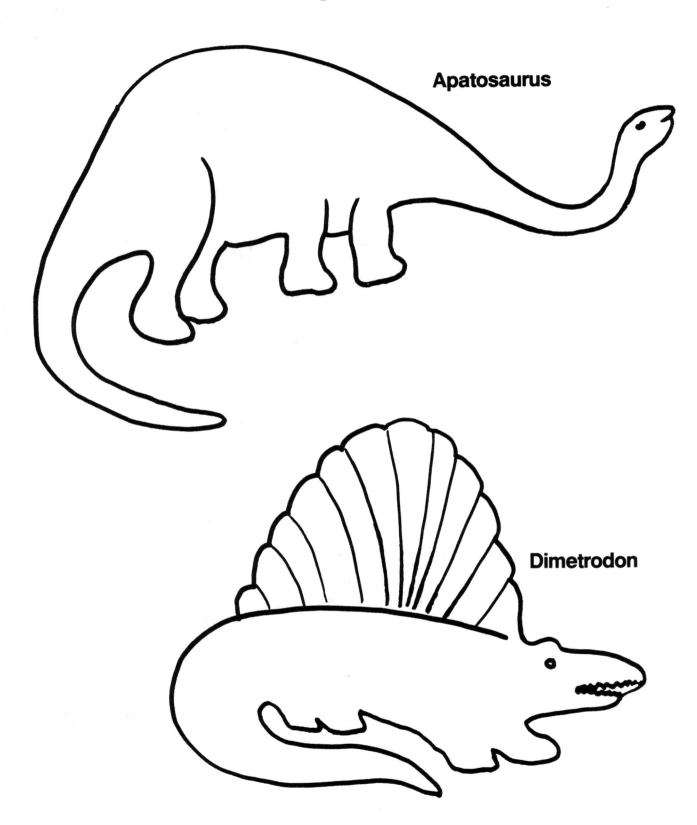

Apatosaurus

Dimetrodon

Dino-myte Patterns

Stegosaurus

Triceratops

Apatosaurus Word Game

How many words can you make from the letters in "Apatosaurus"?

to _____   _____

_____   _____

_____   _____

_____   _____

_____   _____

From *Learning Through Literature,* published by Scott, Foresman and Company.
Copyright © 1991 Mary Jane Butner, Jane Ann Peterson, and Janice Marks Sieplinga.

Name _____

What Did Dinosaurs Eat?

Help us find our favorite food. One of us is an Apatosaurus, a plant-eater. The other is a Tyrannosaurus, a meat-eater.

From *Learning Through Literature*, published by Scott, Foresman and Company.
Copyright © 1991 Mary Jane Butner, Jane Ann Peterson, and Janice Marks Sieplinga.

Stegosaurus Maze

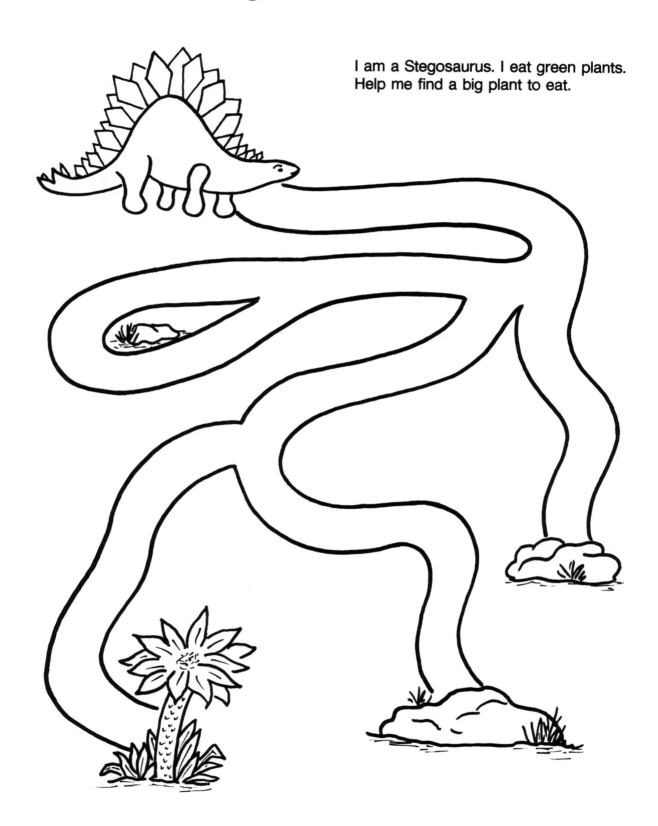

I am a Stegosaurus. I eat green plants. Help me find a big plant to eat.

Dinosaur Match

Draw a line between the dinosaurs that are alike.

DOGS

Clifford the Small Red Puppy, Norman Bridwell, Scholastic Book Services, 1972.

Clifford is so tiny! Will he ever grow? He finally does start to grow . . . and grow . . . and GROW!

Introductory Activity

Surprise Box

Put a bone-shaped dog biscuit inside the surprise box.

Art Activities

Clifford Stick Puppets

Start with a 9-inch square of red construction paper. Fold it into a triangle, fold two corners down for ears, and then draw Clifford's face. Repeat these steps with a 2-inch square of red paper. On a craft stick write: ''Clifford the Small Red Puppy . . .'' On a tongue depressor write: ''became Clifford the Big Red Dog.'' Attach the craft stick and tongue depressor to the appropriate dog puppets.

Paint or Fingerpaint

Give the children red paint to create pictures. You can also give them dog cutouts on which to paint.

*Clifford Hand Puppet

Trace a dog shape on red posterboard. Let the children cut out the shape and add facial features. They can also cut out a tail and attach it with a paper fastener. Staple wide elastic to the back of the puppet.

*Indicates activity that has an accompanying reproducible worksheet.

Tear Paper
Have the children tear red paper and paste it inside a dog shape.

*I Love Clifford

Have the children cut out three hearts and paste two of them upside down to make Clifford's head and body. They can then cut the third heart in half for Clifford's ears and add a tail. Older children may want to write "I Love Clifford."

Language Development

Words to Grow By
While the vocabulary in *Clifford the Small Red Puppy* is minimal, you may want to introduce some of the following words when discussing the story:

big	little
huge	small
large	tiny
enormous	

Something to Think About
What did Emily Elizabeth do to care for Clifford? Why did she choose Clifford, of all the dogs?

What problems would we have if Clifford came to visit us at school?

What problems might you have if you had a dog as big as Clifford?

Do you think a real dog could grow as fast and as big as Clifford? Why or why not?

*Story Map
Use this activity to help the children recall details from the story.

*Indicates activity that has an accompanying reproducible worksheet.

*Is This Clifford?   Challenge the children to list all the differences between the dog in the illustration and Clifford. They should notice, for example, that the dog shown on the worksheet has pointy ears, a short tail, and spots; its eyes and eyebrows are not like Clifford's; and it isn't red.

Find the Bone   Select one child to keep his eyes closed while you hide a bone. Encourage the other children to give clues to help him find it—e. g., "Look high" . . . "You're far away" . . . "Walk towards the window."

All About Dogs   To help the children develop receptive language skills, give them clues that describe dog-related items:

He chews it.	(a bone)
He wears it around his neck.	(a collar)
He scratches at them.	(fleas)
He lives in it.	(a doghouse)
He wears it when going for a walk.	(a leash)
He is very young.	(a puppy)

Toy Dog Show and Tell   Encourage the children to bring some kind of toy dog—or pictures of their real pet dogs—to show.

My Dog Is Special   Make a chart story, using the toy dogs or pictures of real dogs from "Toy Dog Show and Tell." Have each child tell something special about his toy or pet. Older children can write their own stories.

*Structured Story Starter   Have the class help you construct a story about another kind of pet that is unusually large or small. The children choose the animal, designate its color, and give it a name. Challenge them to think about where it would live, what it would eat, what problems it might cause, and what good things it might offer. Older children, after some modeling, can create their own pet stories.

---

*Indicates activity that has an accompanying reproducible worksheet.

Fine and Gross Motor Skills ———————

*Help the Dogs Find Their Bones

Have the children draw lines on the worksheet to help the dogs find their bones—and help themselves develop left-to-right readiness.

*Dogs and Bones

Reproduce these patterns in ten or twelve different colors. Then cut the sheets apart, laminate, and have the children match each dog with its same-colored bone and doghouse.

Dog and Bone Relay

Using the dogs and bones from "Dogs and Bones," give each child a dog and put all the bones together in a pile. Each child must then find a bone to match her dog.

Who's Sitting on the Bone?

Play this game to help the children develop listening and thinking skills. Start by having the children sit in a circle. One child closes his eyes while another child sits on the bone. The first child then opens his eyes, gets up, and starts walking around the circle. When he is far from the person sitting on the bone, the other children bark softly; when he approaches the bone, they bark loudly. Continue the game until everyone has had a turn to search for the bone.

Dog, Dog, Clifford!

Turn "Duck, Duck, Goose" into a canine caper.

*Indicates activity that has an accompanying reproducible worksheet.

From *Learning Through Literature*, published by Scott, Foresman and Company.
Copyright © 1991 Mary Jane Butner, Jane Ann Peterson, and Janice Marks Sieplinga.

Fingerplays and Songs _____

DOGgerel
by Mary Jane Butner

Five snoozing puppies—listen to them snore!
One wakes up, runs off to play; now there are four.
Four curious puppies chase a bumblebee.
Ooops! One gets stung; now there are three.
Three hungry puppies chewing on a shoe.
One sees his supper dish; now there are two.
Two lively puppies—see them jump and run.
One scoots in his doghouse; now there is one.
One small red puppy left, feeling rather lonely.
Emily Elizabeth takes him home; now he's the one and only . . .
CLIFFORD!

Clifford
by Mary Jane Butner, Jane Peterson, Janice Marks Sieplinga
(Tune: "B-I-N-G-O")

Clifford is a big red dog;
I wish he lived at my house.
He could run and fetch a stick.
He could give my face a lick.
I could teach him many tricks,
If Clifford lived at my house.

Clifford is a big red dog;
I wish he lived at my house.
I would show him off with pride—
I couldn't hide him if I tried.
I'd always have him by my side,
If Clifford lived at my house.

Traditional

Oh Where Is My Little Dog Gone?
B-I-N-G-O

_____

*Indicates activity that has an accompanying reproducible worksheet.

Cooking

Canine Cutouts Prepare red finger gelatin and let the children use a donut cutter to make shapes that look like round beef bones.

Clifford Salad

Start with pear halves on lettuce leaves. Add apple slices for ears, raisins for eyes, and a prune for the nose.

Science

Dog Care Talk about pet care with the children. Ask questions such as: What must you do for a dog every day? Why should your dog go to a veterinarian? Why might a dog need shots? Does a dog have special needs during hot weather? cold weather?

Dog Breeds Display books and pictures that show different dog breeds. How many breeds can the children identify? Can they associate specific breeds with special jobs?

Math

*Dog Number Puzzle Trace the pattern onto red posterboard. Cut apart the pieces and challenge the children to put the dog together by placing the numbered pieces in the right order.

*How Many Spots?

Using the "Clifford Hand Puppet" pattern, make ten dogs from red posterboard. Put a different number of spots, from one to ten, on each dog. Number clip clothespins from one to ten. Have the children count each dog's spots and clip on the appropriate clothespin.

---

*Indicates activity that has an accompanying reproducible worksheet.

Graph

Ask the children these questions: Do you have a dog? How many dogs does your family have? Make a graph of their answers.

Extended Experiences _____

Field Trip

Visit a veterinarian.

Canine in the Classroom

Have a parent bring a dog to visit your classroom. The parent should plan to stay and manage the dog throughout its visit.

Related Books _____

Whatever Happens to Puppies? Bill Hall, Golden Press, 1965.
　　This book provides factual information about dogs and their care.

The children will enjoy these other Clifford books by Norman Bridwell, published by Scholastic, Inc.:
Clifford the Big Red Dog, Clifford's Tricks, Clifford's Trip, Clifford's Halloween, Clifford at the Circus, Clifford's Kitten.

*Indicates activity that has an accompanying reproducible worksheet.

From *Learning Through Literature*, published by Scott, Foresman and Company.

Clifford Hand Puppet

add tail

I Love Clifford

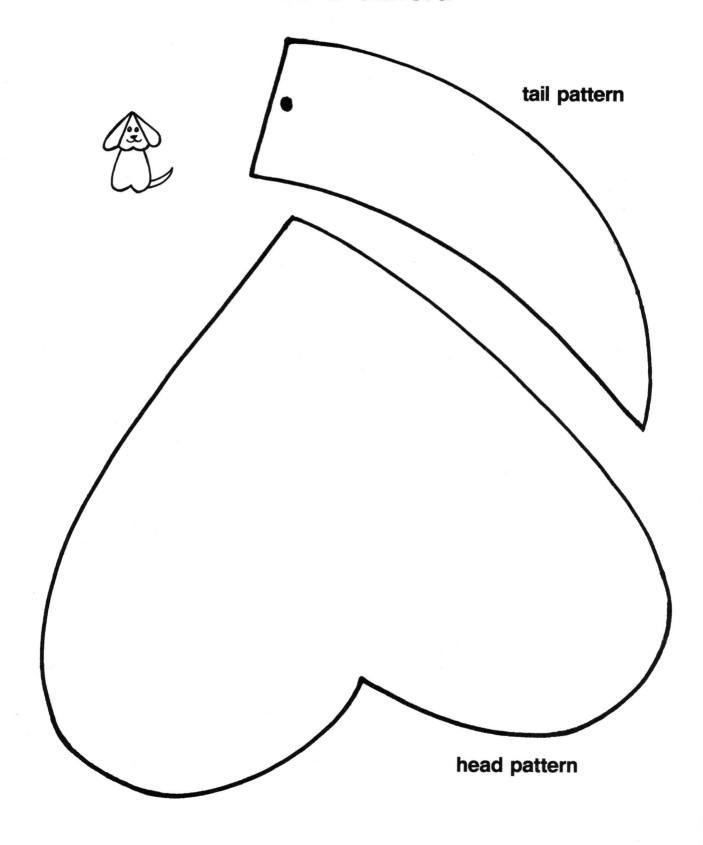

tail pattern

head pattern

I Love Clifford

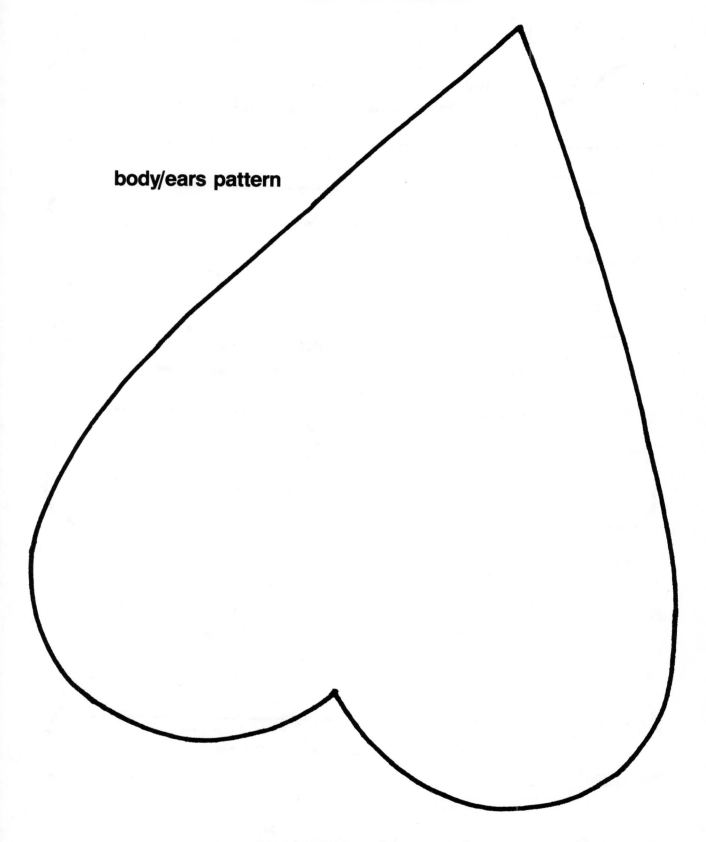

body/ears pattern

Story Map: *Clifford*

What things did Emily need for Clifford?

_____   _____

_____   _____

What people saw Clifford growing?

_____   _____

_____   _____

Where did Emily's family keep Clifford?

_____   _____

_____   _____

From *Learning Through Literature*, published by Scott, Foresman and Company.
Copyright © 1991 Mary Jane Butner, Jane Ann Peterson, and Janice Marks Sieplinga.

Is This Clifford?

Is this a picture of Clifford the big red dog?

No, it is not!

Write some sentences that tell how this dog is different from Clifford.

_____

_____

_____

_____

_____

 Name ______________________________

Structured Story Starter:
Clifford the Small Red Puppy

My pet is a ______________________________

The name of my pet is ______________________________

The color of my pet is ______________________________

My pet is very ______________________________
(big, small, or a synonym for big or small)

This is what happened to me and my pet:

____

____

____

____

____

____

____

____

____

____

____

Name

Help the Dogs Find Their Bones

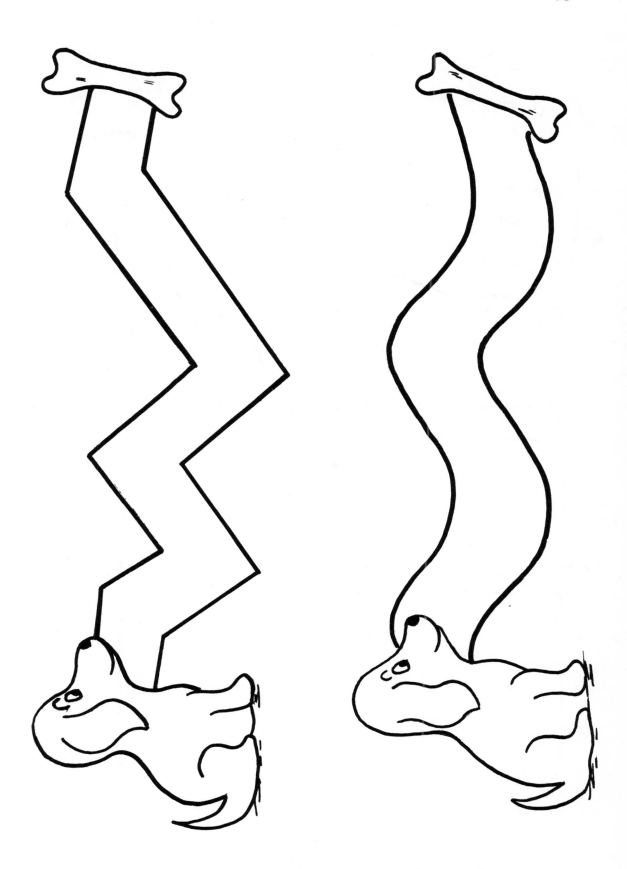

Dogs and Bones

Dog Number Puzzle

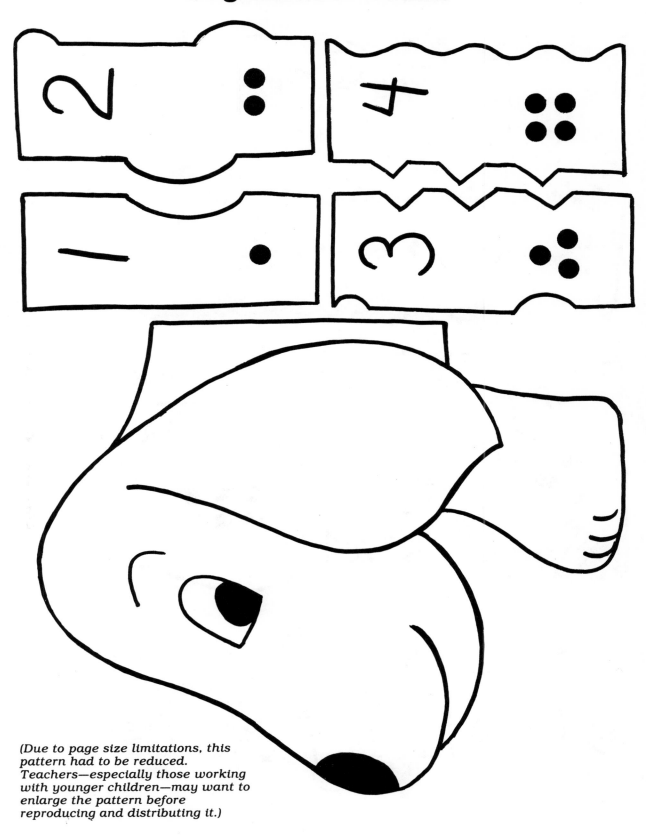

(Due to page size limitations, this pattern had to be reduced. Teachers—especially those working with younger children—may want to enlarge the pattern before reproducing and distributing it.)

Dog Number Puzzle

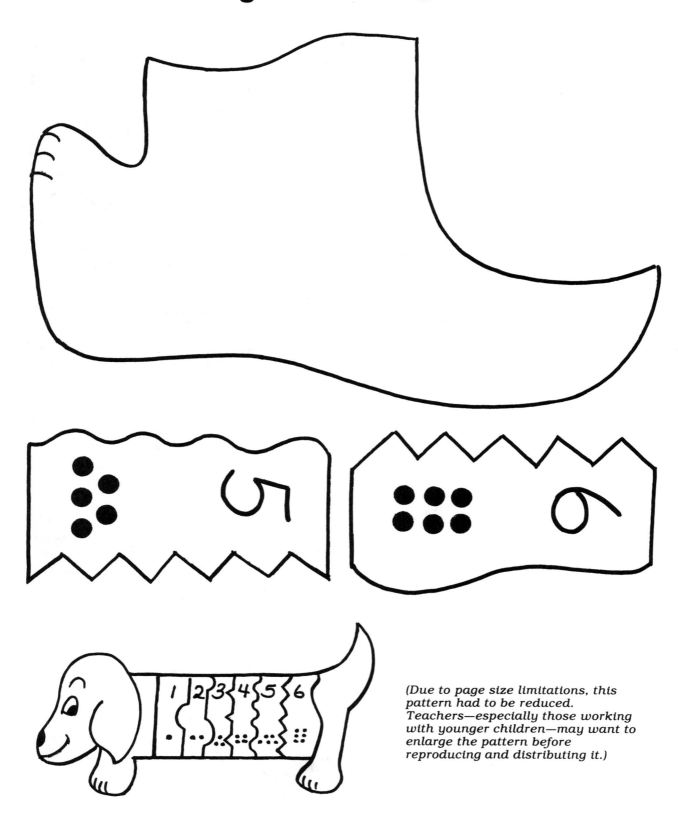

(Due to page size limitations, this pattern had to be reduced. Teachers—especially those working with younger children—may want to enlarge the pattern before reproducing and distributing it.)

DUCKS

Make Way for Ducklings, Robert McCloskey, The Viking Press, 1941.

Mr. and Mrs. Mallard are hunting for a home—never an easy job when there are children to be considered. They eventually find a home in the Boston Public Garden. A Caldecott Award Book.

Introductory Activity

Surprise Box   Place a toy duck, an egg, or a nest in the surprise box.

Art Activities

*Mother Duck and Ducklings   Provide each child with a piece of shelf paper 36 inches long and have the children paste the mother duck (pattern #1) at one end of the paper. Use the sponge paint pattern to cut duck shapes from sponges and have the children sponge paint eight ducklings following the mother duck. If you would rather use 12x18-inch construction paper instead of shelf paper, give the children pattern #2. They can color in waves with a blue crayon before they paint.

Pond Scene   Provide collage material for a pond scene. Give the children sand, blue rick rack for waves, real reeds or grasses, and duck-shaped crackers.

---

*Indicates activity that has an accompanying reproducible worksheet.

Textured Ducks

Choose any one of the duck patterns and let the children produce textured ducks by filling in the outline with yellow cosmetic puffs or with feathers (available at craft stores). The children can also produce textured ducks by rolling small squares of tissue paper on the end of a pencil, dipping the paper in glue, and pressing it into place on the duck outline. Or you can prepare a mixture of powdered detergent and water (beaten to the consistency of whipped cream), add yellow paint, and have the children spread this mixture on the duck pattern.

*Cotton Ball Duckling

Use the pattern provided to make webbed feet out of orange posterboard. Have the children glue two yellow cosmetic puffs (one on top of the other) to the feet, add a beak, and give the duckling eyes made from paper punch dots—or use movable eyes.

*Thumbprint Ducklings

Show the children how to make a thumbprint inside each duckling, using yellow paint. They can then fill in the blanks with the letters J, K, L, M, N, OU, P, and QU to help them remember the names of the ducklings.

Clay or Play Dough

Let the children mold ducks out of these materials. You can also provide cloves for eyes, popsicle sticks for bills, and real feathers.

Language Development

Words to Grow By

mallard
waddled
squawked
dither
Louisburg Square
molt

responsibility
beckoned
Mount Vernon Street
Beacon Street
swan boats

*Indicates activity that has an accompanying reproducible worksheet.

**Something to
Think About**

Where did Mrs. Mallard hatch her ducklings?
Why did Mrs. Mallard decide not to hatch her eggs in the
    Public Garden?
What does "molt" mean?
If Mr. and Mrs. Mallard had had more ducklings, what
    would they have named them?
Which of these places would be good places to raise
    ducklings? Which would not?
        next to the river
        near some railroad tracks
        in the woods
        near a small pond
        in a parking lot
        by a lake
Why didn't Mrs. Mallard want to raise her ducklings near
    foxes or turtles?
Why didn't the swan answer when Mr. Mallard spoke to it?
Why did Mrs. Mallard train her ducklings on the island
    before taking them to the Public Garden?
Do you think Michael likes animals? Can you think of
    some things in the story that prove your answer?

***Flannelboard
Cutouts**

Make eight duckling cutouts and use them to help the
children recall the ducklings' names. In addition, make
cutouts of the nest, mother duck, and eggs to help the
children understand the sequence of the nesting/hatching
cycle.

***Hatching
Ducklings**

You can laminate this worksheet, cut apart the sequence
cards, and use them as a table game. Or you can make
enough copies of the worksheet so that each child can cut
out and paste the pictures in the proper order on a 6x18-
inch strip of paper.

News Flash!

Let the children pretend to be TV reporters telling about
the ducklings' walk on the evening news. Bring in a large
box to use as a TV. Cut out a big square near the top of the
box for the screen. The children can take turns sitting in
the box and acting as TV reporters.

Indicates activity that has an accompanying reproducible worksheet.

*Rhyming Duck

Use this worksheet to introduce the concept of rhyming words. Reproduce on tagboard the duck's head and letter wheel from the patterns on the worksheet. Color, cut out, and fasten the two parts with a paper fastener so that the letters will appear in the duck's open mouth, forming the ducklings' names. The children will enjoy saying the names of the ducklings: Jack, Kack, Lack, Mack, Nack, Ouack, Pack, and Quack.

Rhyming Eggs

Find pictures of items that rhyme, and glue the rhyming pairs on egg shapes. Cut each egg into two parts and challenge the children to reassemble them.

*Story Frame

Use the story frame as a means to check comprehension and recall of details, not as a fill-in-the-blanks activity. Encourage each child to demonstrate independent thought and writing.

Fine and Gross Motor Skills _____

Water Play

Provide toy ducks and let the children make them "dive" in water for food.

*Hidden Ducklings

Challenge the children to find and circle the eight ducklings hidden in the picture.

*Dizzy Duck Maze

Mother Duck swims around and around the maze to find her lost duckling.

*Count the Ducks

Have the children count the ducks. This activity requires children to use their visual discrimination skills in order to separate the overlapping ducks.

Indicates activity that has an accompanying reproducible worksheet.

Duck Walk

Select a child to play "mother duck" for a game of follow the leader. Have the mother duck zigzag, speed up, slow down, etc. Point out that ducklings always follow in a line behind their mother.

Duck Walk Relay

Conduct a relay race in which each child must waddle like a duck.

Duck, Duck, Goose

Of course!

Rhyme Ball

Say a word and then roll a ball to a child who must respond with a rhyming word.

Rhyming Walk

Write beginning sounds—b, bl, cl, cr, r, s, st, sl, t, and tr—on pieces of construction paper or posterboard, and then lay the pieces in a line on the floor. Have the children advance along the path by combining each beginning sound with "_ack."

Fingerplays and Songs

Five Little Ducks
by Mary Jane Butner

Five little ducks swimming by the shore
One waddled home and then there were four.
Four little ducks swimming out to sea
One stopped to catch a fish and then there were three.
Three little ducks in the water so blue
One heard his mother call and then there were two.
Two little ducks having lots of fun
One went home for supper and then there was one.
One little duck said, "My friends have all run.
I'll go home too and then there'll be none!"

Indicates activity that has an accompanying reproducible worksheet.

From *Learning Through Literature*, published by Scott, Foresman and Company.
Copyright © 1991 Mary Jane Butner, Jane Ann Peterson, and Janice Marks Sieplinga.

The Ducklings
First Verse, Traditional
Second Verse, Jane Peterson

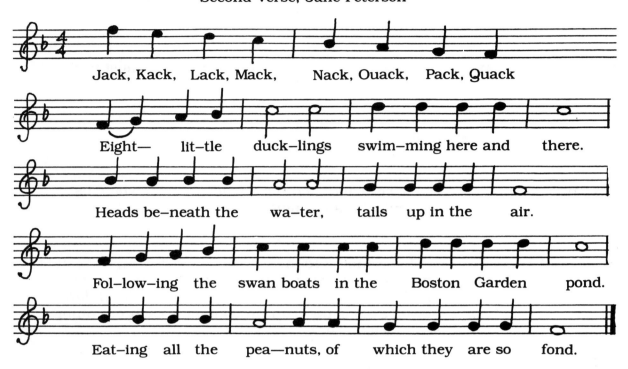

Jack, Kack, Lack, Mack,   Nack, Ouack,   Pack, Quack

Eight—   lit–tle   duck–lings   swim–ming here and   there.

Heads be–neath the   wa–ter,   tails   up in the   air.

Fol–low–ing   the   swan boats   in the   Boston   Garden   pond.

Eat–ing   all   the   pea—nuts, of   which they   are so   fond.

Cooking _____

Ducks on a Log

In this variation on an old favorite, let the children spread peanut butter or cream cheese on a piece of celery and then stand several duck-shaped crackers in it.

Indicates activity that has an accompanying reproducible worksheet.

Science _____

*Mr. and Mrs. Mallard

This color by number activity will help the children see the differences between the male and female mallards.

Which Came First?

Try to obtain chicken, duck, turkey, and goose eggs from a farmer and let the children observe and compare sizes, colors, and markings.

Birds and Fowl

Collect books and pictures that show birds and fowl. Tell the children to look carefully at the animals' shapes, beaks, and feet, noting any similarities and differences. You may want to ask the children why ducks have webbed feet, why some birds have sharp beaks, etc.

Math _____

*Flannelboard Math

Use the flannelboard cutouts of eggs and ducklings to develop one-to-one correspondence—i. e., one duckling will hatch out of each egg. After putting up three eggs, have a child count them and add the corresponding number of ducklings. Repeat the activity several times with other numbers.

*Duck, Duck, Gone!

Use the cutouts of the ducklings and eggs to do some flannelboard addition and subtraction.

Graph

Ask the children, ''Have you seen baby ducklings?'' Each child answers by clipping a clothespin to the yes pond or the no pond (made from construction paper). Count and compare the responses.

---

*Indicates activity that has an accompanying reproducible worksheet.

Extended Experiences ⎯⎯⎯⎯⎯⎯⎯⎯⎯⎯⎯⎯⎯⎯⎯

Field Trip   Visit a poultry farm.

Feed the Ducks   Take a walk to a nearby duck pond, and take along some
                          bread to feed the ducks.

Related Books ⎯⎯⎯⎯⎯⎯⎯⎯⎯⎯⎯⎯⎯⎯⎯⎯⎯⎯

The children will enjoy reading about these other adventurous ducks:
The Fuzzy Duckling, Jane Werner, Golden Press, Western Publishing
Company, Inc., 1949.
Have You Seen My Duckling? Nancy Tafuri, Greenwillow Books, 1984.
The Runaway Duck, David Lyon, Mulberry Books, 1985.
The Story About Ping, Marjorie Flack, The Viking Press, 1933.

Indicates activity that has an accompanying reproducible worksheet.

Mother Duck and Ducklings

pattern #1

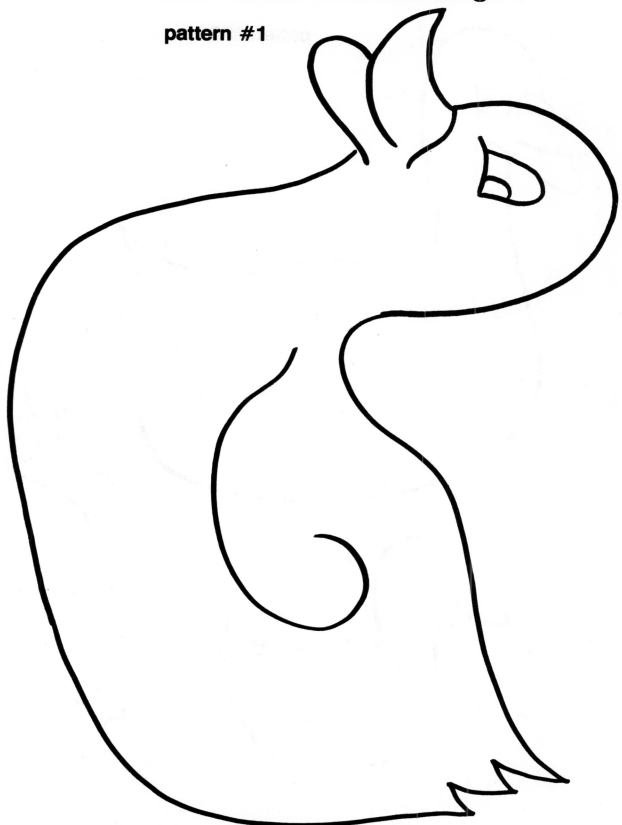

Mother Duck and Ducklings

pattern #2

Mother Duck and Ducklings

sponge paint pattern

Cotton Ball Duckling

68

From *Learning Through Literature*, published by Scott, Foresman and Company.
Copyright © 1991 Mary Jane Butner, Jane Ann Peterson, and Janice Marks Sieplinga.

Thumbprint Ducklings

_____ ack

_____ ack

_____ ack

_____ ack

_____ ack

_____ ack

_____ ack

_____ ack

Flannelboard Cutouts

make 8
of each

Hatching Ducklings

Rhyming Duck

Story Frame:
Make Way for Ducklings

Mr. and Mrs. Mallard needed to find _____

_____

They liked the Boston Public Garden, but _____

_____

At last they settled down _____

_____

Mrs. Mallard taught her babies _____

_____

Finally, she thought they were ready to _____

_____

Michael helped the ducks by _____

_____

At the end of the story, _____

_____

From *Learning Through Literature*, published by Scott, Foresman and Company.
Copyright © 1991 Mary Jane Butner, Jane Ann Peterson, and Janice Marks Sieplinga.

Name

Hidden Ducklings

Help Mother Duck find her eight ducklings.

Dizzy Duck Maze

Help Mother Duck find her duckling.

Count the Ducks

Name _____

Mr. and Mrs. Mallard

1. white
2. yellow
3. green
4. orange (rust)
5. tan
6. blue
7. dark brown
8. black
9. gray

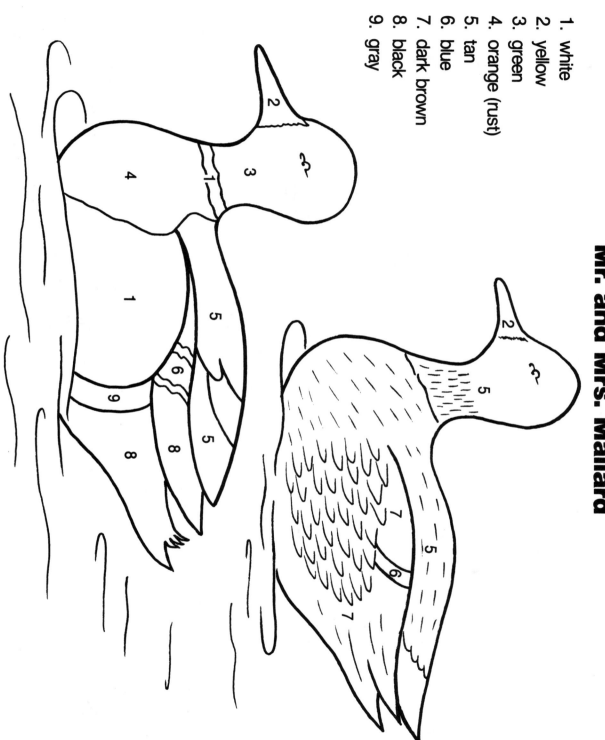

MICE

Frederick, Leo Lionni, Pantheon Books, 1967.
Some mice store up nuts and berries for the winter.
Frederick is different: he stores up words and colors for
winter warmth and comfort. A Caldecott Honor Book.

Introductory Activity

Surprise Box   Put a toy mouse, some corn, or nuts in the surprise box.

Art Activities

Shape Mouse

Have the children cut out a half circle for the mouse's body, a triangle for the head, and two small circles for the ears. They can add a yarn tail and paper scraps for feet.

Paper Plate Mouse

Have each child paint a paper plate gray and then add circle ears and facial features.

Frederick

The children can cut out a dark gray oval, add light gray circle ears and a yarn tail, and use a black crayon to draw facial features and legs. They can paste their Frederick on a multicolored background, made by randomly rubbing peeled crayons over paper.

Egg Carton Mouse

Have each child paint one section of an egg carton gray, then add a yarn tail and construction paper features.

*Indicates activity that has an accompanying reproducible worksheet.

Nature Collage   Go for a nature walk and collect a variety of items along
                            the way. Back in the classroom, give the children
                            Styrofoam meat trays to which they can glue the nature
                            items.

*Nutshell and Seed   Show the children how to make prints using walnut,
Prints   pecan, or peanut shells. Dip the shells in paint and press
                            onto paper that has been cut into a nut shape. You can
                            also use apricot pits and peach stones for this activity;
                            their textured surfaces, when dipped in paint, make
                            interesting designs.

Language Development _____

Words to Grow By   meadow   nibbled
                            granary   supplies
                            abandoned   applauded
                            reproachfully

Something to   Why were the mice working so hard?
Think About   Why did they need so much food?
                            If you had to gather supplies for the whole winter, what
                                would you include?
                            Compare what the mice did to get ready for winter with
                                what you and your family do.
                            Who do you think did the most important work—Frederick
                                or the other mice?

*Getting Ready for   Have the children draw lines between the descriptions and
Winter Riddles   the appropriate pictures.

Word List   Ask each child to tell her favorite word, the biggest word
                            she knows, or the one with the most interesting sound.
                            Record the responses on chart paper.

_____

*Indicates activity that has an accompanying reproducible worksheet.

*Frederick Word Game

The children can make names for the other mice from the letters in Frederick's name (Ed, Fred, Keri, Dee, Rick, Dick, Derek, Eric, Red, Fredi, Di).

Word Savers

Put a picture of Frederick on a bulletin board, and then add a collection of nut shapes cut out of paper. As the children learn new words, they can print the words on the "nuts" for Frederick to store. For beginning readers, put recognized words on cards so that each child can keep sight words in a word bank.

*Story Frame

The story frame activity helps children recall details and identify the main idea of the story. Not simply a "fill-in-the-blanks" activity, it requires the use of writing skills.

Fine and Gross Motor Skills

*Help the Mice

By helping the mice carry nuts and grains to store by the rocks, the children get practice in left-to-right readiness.

Picking Up Nuts

Scatter pegs, bingo markers, acorns, or popcorn kernels on the floor. Give each child a bag. Wind up a music box and see how many objects the children can pick up before the music stops.

Cat and Mouse

Gather the children in a circle and show them two balls of different sizes. Explain that the larger ball is the cat while the smaller ball is the mouse. Start passing the smaller ball around the circle and then start the larger ball a few seconds later. Have the children continue passing them until the cat catches up with the mouse.

*Count the Acorns

Have the children count the acorns on the worksheet. This activity requires the children to use visual discrimination skills in order to separate the acorns for counting.

Indicates activity that has an accompanying reproducible worksheet.

From *Learning Through Literature*, published by Scott, Foresman and Company.
Copyright © 1991 Mary Jane Butner, Jane Ann Peterson, and Janice Marks Sieplinga.

Fingerplays and Songs _____

Frederick and the Field Mice
by Mary Jane Butner

See the little field mice storing nuts away
On a warm September day.

But Frederick stores colors and words in his den;
When winter comes, he'll take them out again.

See the little field mice carrying corn
On a cool October morn.

But Frederick stores colors and words in his den;
When winter comes, he'll take them out again.

See the little field mice gathering grain
In the cold November rain.

But Frederick stores colors and words in his den;
When winter comes, he'll take them out again.

Little Mice
by Janice Marks Sieplinga
(Tune: "Farmer in the Dell")

The mice go out to play,
The mice go out to play.
Watch out for the old gray cat,
While you're out to play.

The mice find the corn,
The mice find the corn.
Watch out for the old gray cat,
While you find the corn.

The little mice all run,
The little mice all run.
The old gray cat has caught a mouse.
The little mice all run.

*Indicates activity that has an accompanying reproducible worksheet.

Mice
by Janice Sieplinga
(Tune: "This Old Man")

Five little mice go out to play,
Gathering corn along the way.
Out comes the curious old gray cat.
Four little mice go scampering back.

(Repeat the verse, counting down four, three, two, one.)

Cooking _____

Mouse Nibblies   Put out a selection of cereals, nuts, dried fruits, carob chips, and sunflower seeds. Give the children small bowls and let them create their own snacks from these nutritious foods.

Corny Kernels   If cooking facilities are available, the children may enjoy fixing corn on the cob.

Science _____

Cold Weather Preparation   Talk about what different animals do to get ready for winter.

Discovering Seeds—1   Bring in several seeds with which the children are not familiar. Put the seeds on a table along with the real fruits and vegetables that the seeds grow into. Let individuals or small groups cut open the fruits and vegetables (under adult supervision!) and then try to match the seeds inside with the ones already on the table.

Indicates activity that has an accompanying reproducible worksheet.

From *Learning Through Literature*, published by Scott, Foresman and Company.
Copyright © 1991 Mary Jane Butner, Jane Ann Peterson, and Janice Marks Sieplinga.

Discovering Seeds—2

Bring in two seeds each for a variety of fruits. Glue one of each pair on a card with a picture of the appropriate fruit on the other side; glue the matching seed on another card. Have the child match the seed card with the picture of the fruit. He can easily check his work by turning over the picture card to see if the two seeds match.

Tasting Dried Fruits

Let the children compare the tastes and textures of fresh and dried fruits. For example, you can give them grapes and raisins, plums and prunes, and both fresh and dried slices of apricots, apples, and pineapple.

Math

Numbering With Nuts

Have the children collect whatever autumn nuts are available in your area. Use these nuts for a variety of activities: counting, doing addition or subtraction facts, comparing sizes and weights, etc.

Extended Experiences

Field Trip

Take a trip to a nature center or to some woods or a meadow. Look for signs of autumn and talk about what the animals are doing to prepare for winter. Collect nature items in lunch bags.

Related Books

Whose Mouse Are You? Robert Kraus, The MacMillan Company, 1970.
    Poor lonely mouse—can he bring his family together and be somebody's mouse?

The Wonders of the Season, Bertha Morris Parker, Western Publishing Company, 1966.
    This book contains beautiful pictures that show the seasonal changes.

*Indicates activity that has an accompanying reproducible worksheet.

Nutshell and Seed Prints

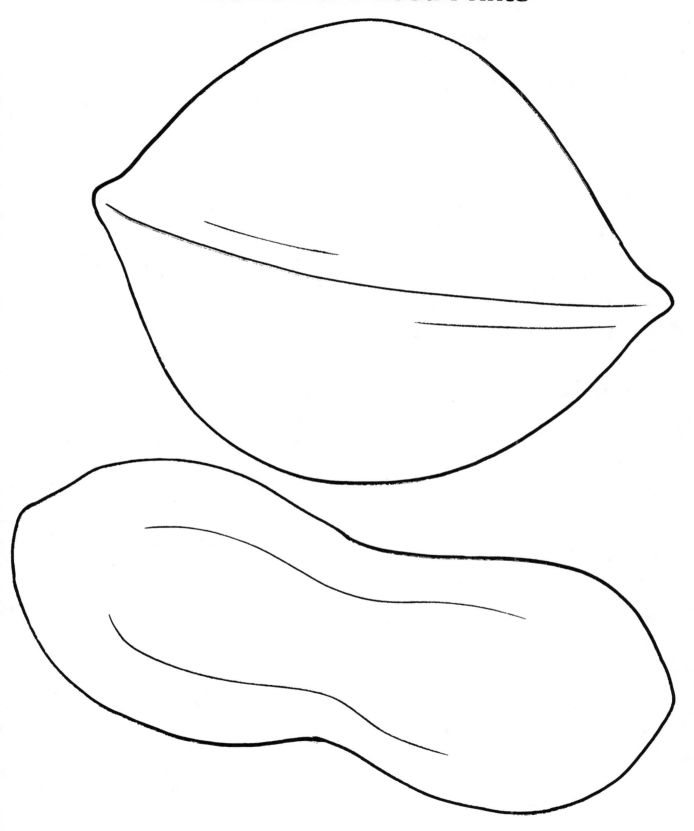

Getting Ready for Winter Riddles

I fly to where it's warmer.

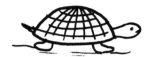

I dig down into the mud to sleep.

I get out my snowsuit and mittens.

I gather acorns.

I go to sleep in my cave.

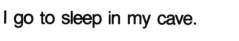

Frederick Word Game

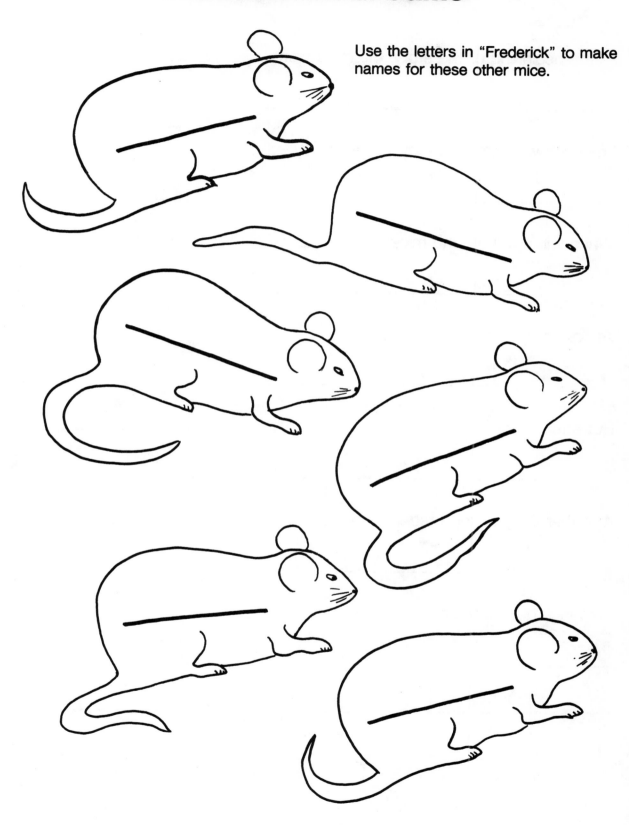

Use the letters in "Frederick" to make names for these other mice.

Story Frame: *Frederick*

At the beginning of the story, the mice were _____

_____

Frederick was getting ready for winter by _____

_____

When winter came, the mice _____

_____

At first, they had _____

_____

But after awhile _____

_____

And then they asked Frederick to _____

_____

Frederick helped the other mice to feel_____

_____

_____

Name _____

Help the Mice

Help the mice store food by the rock.

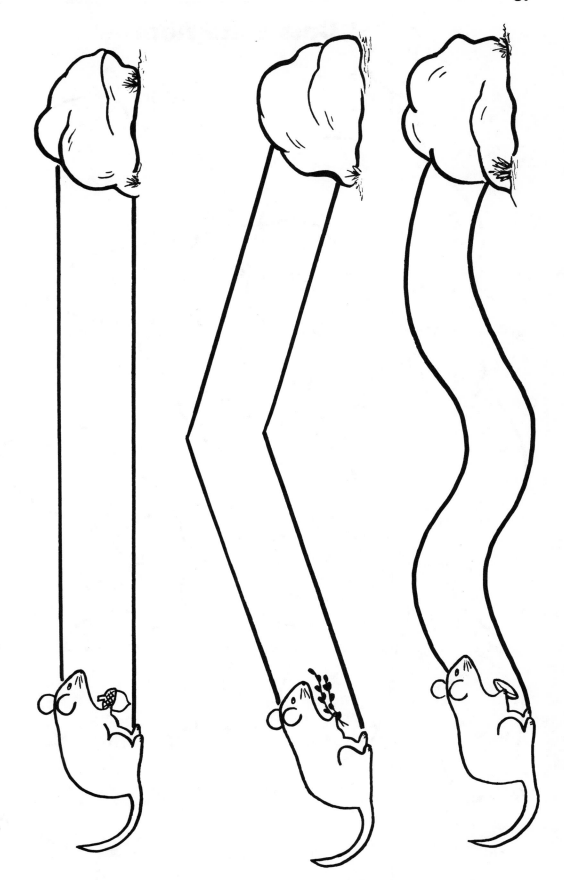

Count the Acorns

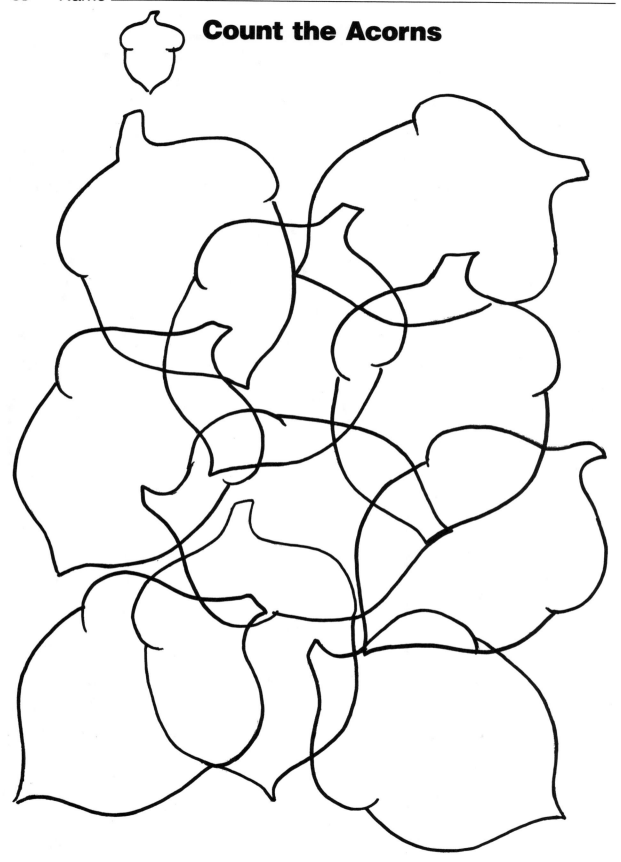

MONKEYS

Caps for Sale, Esphyr Slobodkina, Harper Trophy Book, Harper and Row, 1987.
A peddler loses his caps to some monkeys. How can he get them back? "Monkey see, monkey do!"

Introductory Activity

Surprise Box   Put a stuffed monkey, a hat, or a cap in the surprise box.

Art Activities

Make a Funny Hat

Provide paper plates, glue, yarn, tissue, crepe paper, scraps of material, etc., and let the children exercise their imaginations in making original hat designs.

*Self-Portrait With Hat   Have each child draw a self-portrait and then cut out and paste on one of the pre-drawn hats from the worksheet.

*Peddler and Caps

Give each child a 6x18-inch piece of construction paper with an oval drawn at the bottom. Have the children draw the peddler's face—including the mustache! Reproduce the cap pattern on brown, blue, gray, and red construction paper, providing the children with many caps of each color. Some children may want to cut out many caps; others will want to cut out just one of each color. Have the children paste the caps on the peddler's head—Caps for Sale!

*Indicates activity that has an accompanying reproducible worksheet.

Newspaper Hats

Show the children how to fold a sheet of newspaper to form a hat. They can then decorate their hats with scraps of paper, color-coding labels, feathers, etc.

1. Begin with a full sheet of newspaper (2 pages, approximately 14x24 inches).

2. Fold the top of the sheet down to the bottom, forming a 12x14-inch rectangle.

3. Fold the top left corner into the center, forming a right triangle.

4. Repeat step 3 with the top right corner.

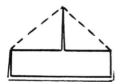

5. Fold the bottom of the newspaper sheet up to meet the base of the triangle, and then fold it up once again.

6. Turn the folded newspaper over and repeat on the back side.

7. Staple or tape the ends of the hat brim.

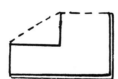

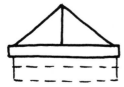

---

*Indicates activity that has an accompanying reproducible worksheet.

Language Development _____

Words to Grow By   peddler   ordinary
                         wares   disturb
                         refreshed

**Something to
Think About**
How much did the peddler's caps cost?
What was unusual about the peddler?
Why did the monkeys finally give the hats back to the
    peddler?
If a monkey had one of your mittens, how might you get it
    back?
Tell how the monkeys in this story are like Curious George.
How can the peddler convince a person he meets to buy
    one of his caps?
Would it be easier to sell things by going to people's homes
    or by working in a store? Why?

**Favorite Hat Show
and Tell**
Encourage each child to wear a favorite hat to school and
tell why it is special.

Pantomime
Have each child pretend to shop for a new hat by trying on
many hats in front of a mirror.

Who Wears It?
Show pictures of various hats—e. g., cowboy, sailor, fire
helmet, construction hardhat, engineer's cap—that are
associated with specific jobs. Ask the children to describe
the kind of people who wear each of the hats and
something about the work they do.

Indicates activity that has an accompanying reproducible worksheet.

1-2-3 Look and See

Using the hat pictures from the "Who Wears It?" activity, lay out three to five pictures for the children to study. Then have the children close their eyes. While they have their eyes closed, take away one of the pictures. The children open their eyes and tell which hat is missing. Repeat the activity several times, using a different picture each time.

Which Hat Is It?

Tape one of the hat pictures from the "Who Wears It?" activity to the back of a child's shirt. Let the other children see which hat it is. Then have the children give clues—e.g., "You put out fires" . . . "You build things" . . . "You work on a ship"—until the child with the picture guesses what kind of worker she is supposed to be.

Dramatization

Children love to act out *Caps for Sale*, imitating the peddler and the monkeys. With very young children, the teacher can act as the peddler.

*Story Frame

A story frame helps children recall details and identify the main idea of a story. Not simply a fill-in-the-blanks activity, it requires the use of thinking and writing skills.

Fine and Gross Motor Skills

*Trace Some Hats

Give the children some practice in developing eye-hand coordination by having them trace around the hats.

Puzzles

You can buy a wooden inlay puzzle with occupational hats or make your own out of posterboard. Limit the hat puzzle to two or three pieces, and draw an outline on another piece of posterboard as a guide for doing the puzzle.

*Indicates activity that has an accompanying reproducible worksheet.

Beanbag Activities   Let the children pretend to be the peddler by balancing one or more beanbags on their heads while walking around, sitting down, standing up, turning around, and calling out "Caps for sale!"

Monkey See,   In this follow-the-leader game, let each child initiate an
Monkey Do   activity for the other children to imitate.

Fingerplays and Songs _____

Monkeys and Caps
by Mary Jane Butner

Five little monkeys sitting in a tree,
Along came a peddler, and what did he see?
"Hey! You naughty monkeys! Those caps belong to me!"
A monkey threw a cap down and jumped from the tree.

(Repeat the verse with four, three, two, and one.)

Whose Hat?
by Jane Peterson
(Tune: "The Muffin Man")

Oh, do you know whose hat this is?
Whose hat this is, whose hat this is?
Oh, do you know whose hat this is?
It belongs to the fireman.

(Repeat the verse with policeman, mailman, nurse, etc.)

_____

Indicates activity that has an accompanying reproducible worksheet.

Caps for Sale
by Mary Jane Butner

Up and down, round and round, A ped—dler walked all through the town.

Sing—ing, "Caps for sale! Caps for sale! Fif—ty cents a cap!"

(Action Chorus: Encourage the children to perform the actions—make a fist, stamp their feet, shake a finger—as they sing the chorus.)

Make a fist and stamp your feet, Shake your fin—ger if you meet—

A ped—dler sing—ing, "Caps for sale! Fif—ty cents a cap!"

Caps of red, caps of blue,
Gray ones, brown ones, white ones, too.
The peddler lost those caps for sale—
Fifty cents a cap! (Action chorus)

The peddler looked up in a tree;
What do you think that he could see?
Monkeys wearing caps for sale—
Fifty cents a cap! (Action chorus)

Caps of red, caps of blue,
Gray ones, brown ones, white ones, too.
The monkeys threw down caps for sale—
Fifty cents a cap! (Action chorus)

Traditional   *My Hat, It Has Three Corners*

Indicates activity that has an accompanying reproducible worksheet.

From *Learning Through Literature*, published by Scott, Foresman and Company.

Cooking

Banana Bread   Help the children make banana bread, using a packaged quick bread mix.

Science

Primate Panorama   Show the children a variety of pictures of monkeys, apes, chimpanzees, and gorillas. How are they the same? How are they different?

The Real Thing   Wouldn't it be fun to have a *real* monkey or chimp visit the class?!! Call your local zoo and see if such a visit can be arranged.

Math

*Monkeys and Caps   Use the patterns to make monkeys and caps out of posterboard. Put numbers on the monkeys and a corresponding number of dots on the caps. Let the children match up each monkey with its cap.

Extended Experiences

Field Trip   Plan a field trip to a pet store that handles monkeys or to a zoo. You might also take the class to a millinery shop.

Indicates activity that has an accompanying reproducible worksheet.

From *Learning Through Literature*, published by Scott, Foresman and Company.
Copyright © 1991 Mary Jane Butner, Jane Ann Peterson, and Janice Marks Sieplinga.

Related Books ―――――――――――――――――――――――――――

Old Hat, New Hat, Stan and Jan Berenstain, Random House, 1970.
An easy reader, this book features a bear who tries on every hat in the store before finding the perfect one—his own!

Jennie's Hat, Ezra Jack Keats, Harper and Row, 1966.
Jennie's aunt sends her a hat that is disappointingly plain.

Indicates activity that has an accompanying reproducible worksheet.

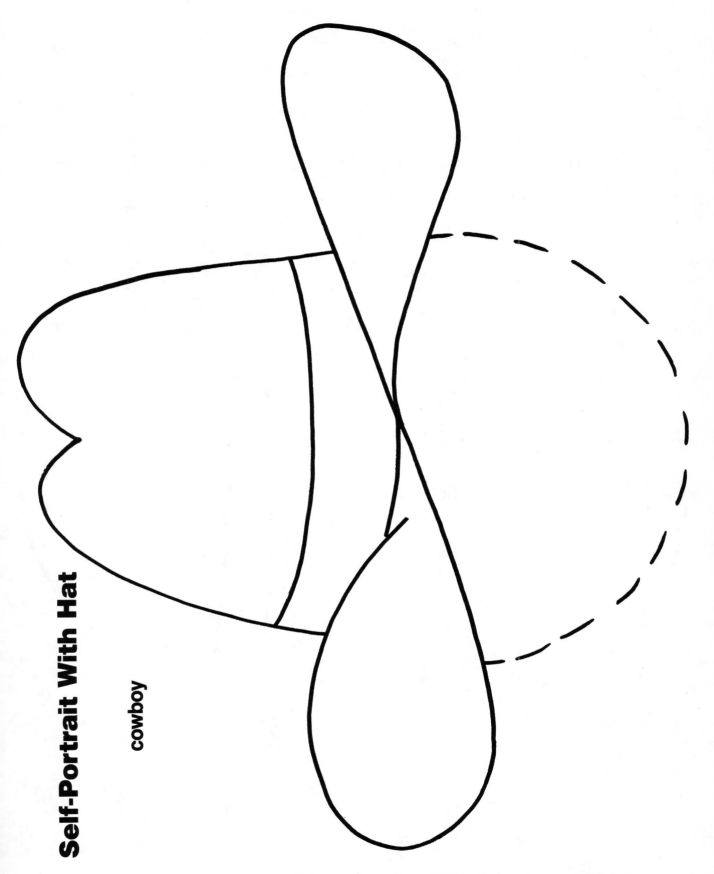

Self-Portrait With Hat

cowboy

Self-Portrait With Hat

bonnet
(add a flower or feather)

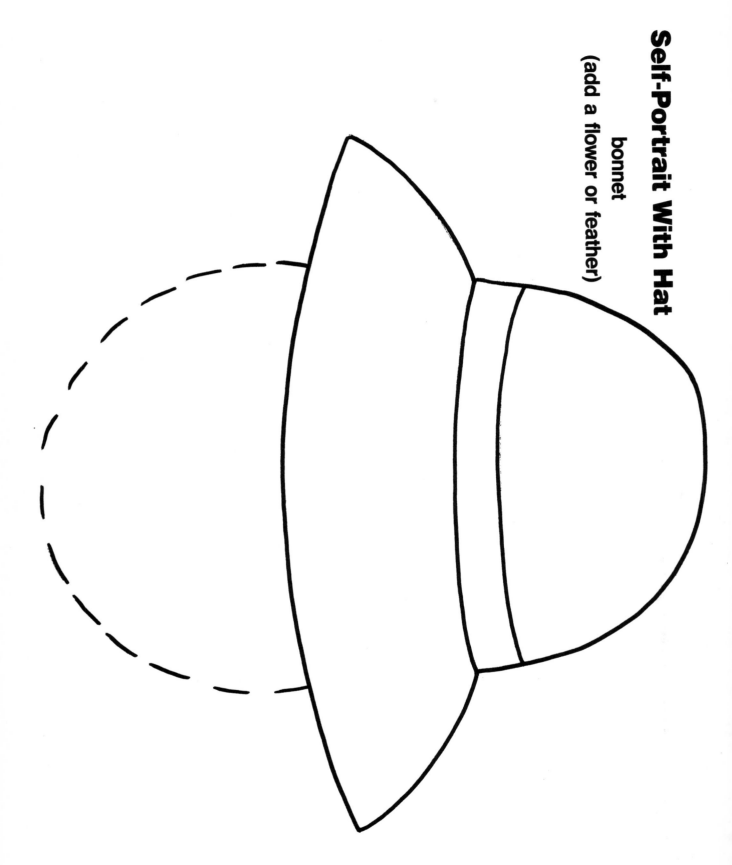

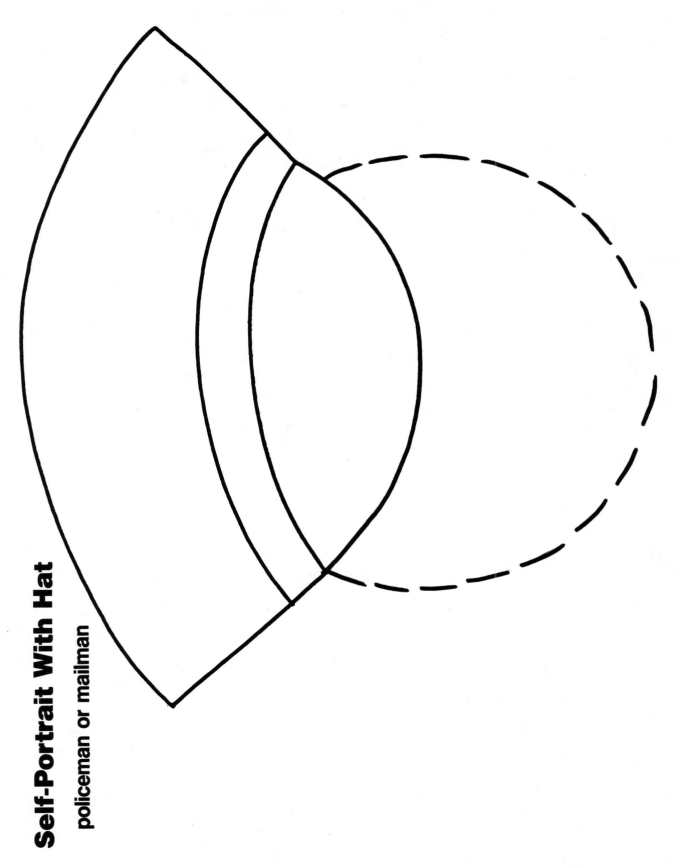

Self-Portrait With Hat

policeman or mailman

Peddler and Caps

Monkeys and Caps

monkey's cap

make in many colors (also checked, like the peddler's)

2

Story Frame: *Caps for Sale*

This story is about a man who _____

_____

Every day, he _____

_____

One day, he could not _____

_____

He went for a walk because _____

_____

After he walked out of the town, _____

_____

After his nap, he _____

_____

He couldn't get the monkeys to _____

_____

They finally gave him the caps when _____

_____

Trace Some Hats

MONKEYS

Curious George, H. A. Rey, Houghton Mifflin, 1941.
   Children enjoy the antics of this funny little monkey. In this,
   the first of the series, George's curiosity gets him into trouble
   with the fire department and a balloon man.

Introductory Activity

Surprise Box   Put a toy telephone, a balloon, or a stuffed animal of
                          Curious George (available in many toy stores) in the
                          surprise box.

Art Activities

*Monkey Mask

The children cut out the mask—including the center
section—and put on gummed reinforcements to strengthen
the holes before attaching the strings. When the children
wear the masks, their faces become monkey faces!

***Monkey Hand
Puppet**

Reproduce the pattern on brown construction paper. Then
let the children cut two patterns each and lace around the
edges. Remind the children to leave the bottom open.

*(The following art activities are based on incidents in the story.
You may want to have older children write sentences describing
what has happened to George after they finish each project.)*

---

*Indicates activity that has an accompanying reproducible worksheet.

*Monkey Under a Hat

Give each child a copy of the monkey picture to color. Reproduce the hat on yellow construction paper. The children cut out the hat and attach it to the monkey with a paper fastener.

*Monkey and Balloons

Reproduce the pattern on brown construction paper. The children cut out the monkey and the arms, attach the arms with a paper fastener (positioning them upward), and paste the monkey on a 12x18-inch sheet of construction paper. Then they draw balloons with strings for the monkey to hold.

Language Development

Words to Grow By

curious
Africa
fascinated

signal
whisked
gusts

Something to Think About

What kinds of trouble did George get into?
What does the word "curious" mean?
Why did George try to fly like the sea gulls?
Think of some times when curiosity is good and times when it can lead to trouble.
Tell why the zoo might or might not be a good place for George to live.

*Structured Story Starter

Have the children help you construct a story about another kind of curious animal and an owner who parallels "the man with the yellow hat." After some modeling, older children can create their own curious animal stories.

*Story Map

This activity will help the children recall the who, what, and where of *Curious George.*

*Indicates activity that has an accompanying reproducible worksheet.

| **Telephone Talk** | Let two children at a time use toy telephones to demonstrate good telephone manners. |

Telephone Talk Let two children at a time use toy telephones to demonstrate good telephone manners.

Take a Message Pretend to call a child on the toy phone, and give her a message to repeat to another child.

Telephone Play the old game in which one person whispers a message and the listener passes it to someone else, and so on, until the last person repeats the message out loud. The children will enjoy hearing how the message gets changed as it is passed along!

Fine and Gross Motor Skills

***Help the Monkey** By tracing a path from the monkey to the hat, telephone, and bunch of balloons, the children get good practice in left-to-right readiness.

***Monkey Maze** This activity will help develop tracking, small muscle control, and decision-making skills.

Take a Message Modify the language development activity so that your messages are instructions to do large muscle tasks—e. g., "Tell Matt to hop on one foot. Tell Glenn to tiptoe to the table."

Monkey See, Monkey Do Choose one child to be the leader (the monkey). He stands in front of the group and performs a simple action. Everyone chants, "Monkey see, monkey do!" and they imitate the leader's action. Let each child have a turn as leader. As a variation on the basic game, challenge the children by telling them that their actions must involve a specific body part.

*Indicates activity that has an accompanying reproducible worksheet.

From *Learning Through Literature*, published by Scott, Foresman and Company. Copyright © 1991 Mary Jane Butner, Jane Ann Peterson, and Janice Marks Sieplinga.

Balance Beam   Ask the children to tiptoe across a balance beam—as George tiptoed on the telephone wires to escape from prison.

Fingerplays and Songs ────────────────────

Five Little Monkeys

This poem is always popular with young children. They can do it with finger motions only, or they can act it out by playing the jumping monkeys, mother, and doctor.

Because He Was Curious!
by Mary Jane Butner and Jane Ann Peterson
(Tune: "Pop Goes the Weasel")

One day a man with a big yellow hat
Found a cute little monkey.
The monkey got into mischief—and more—
Because he was curious!

George wanted to soar like the gulls;
He zoomed into the air,
Then plummeted to the ocean beneath—
Because he was curious!

George wanted to use the telephone;
He called the fire station.
The firemen answered a false alarm—
Because George was curious!

George tiptoed on the telephone wire;
He came upon a balloon man.
The balloons lifted him high in the air!
Because he was curious!

───

Indicates activity that has an accompanying reproducible worksheet.

Cooking _____

Banana Treat   Let the children peel bananas and cut them into pieces. Heat a jar of fudge sauce. Then let the children dip their banana pieces in the chocolate.

Science _____

Paper Cup Telephones   Punch small holes in the bottoms of two plastic cups, push string through, and tie it inside the cups. With the string stretched tight, a child talks into one of the cups while another listens with the other cup to her ear.

The Important Thumb   Challenge the children to try various tasks (writing, picking up objects, holding a cup, or stringing beads) without using their thumbs. You might try taping their thumbs to their palms so they won't be tempted to use them, but don't insist on taping if the children object. Young children sometimes become frightened or upset at being bound in any way.

Monkeys and Apes   Display books that contain pictures of different kinds of monkeys and apes.

Math _____

Five Little Monkeys   This favorite poem involves counting and subtraction. Make flannelboard cutouts for the children to count as the monkeys fall off the bed. You might even start with more than five monkeys and challenge the children to see how many are left as two, three, or more fall off the bed at the same time.

Indicates activity that has an accompanying reproducible worksheet.

All Thumbs

Have the children count the thumbs of everyone in the class: all the girls' thumbs, all the boys' thumbs, all left thumbs, all right thumbs. Then present some math questions like these:

If Jonathan and Andrew are playing, and Paul and Jan join them, how many thumbs will there be?

Seven children are playing, but then Greg and Nicholas go home. How many thumbs are left after they leave?

If you can see ten thumbs, how many people must there be?

Extended Experiences

Field Trip

Go on a field trip to the zoo or to a pet shop that handles monkeys.

Resource Person

Try to track down someone who has a pet monkey or chimpanzee and will agree to bring it on a visit to the class.

Related Books

Children will enjoy the further adventures of Curious George in these other books by H. A. Rey:
Curious George Flies a Kite, Curious George Gets a Medal, Curious George Takes a Job, Curious George Goes to the Hospital, Curious George Rides a Bike, Curious George Learns the Alphabet.
In addition, there are some newer books (edited by Margaret Rey and Alan J. Shalleck) based on the Curious George film series. Offering fairly easy reading for beginning readers, these books have colorful pictures and only one or two sentences on a page.

Indicates activity that has an accompanying reproducible worksheet.

From *Learning Through Literature,* published by Scott, Foresman and Company.
Copyright © 1991 Mary Jane Butner, Jane Ann Peterson, and Janice Marks Sieplinga.

Monkey Mask

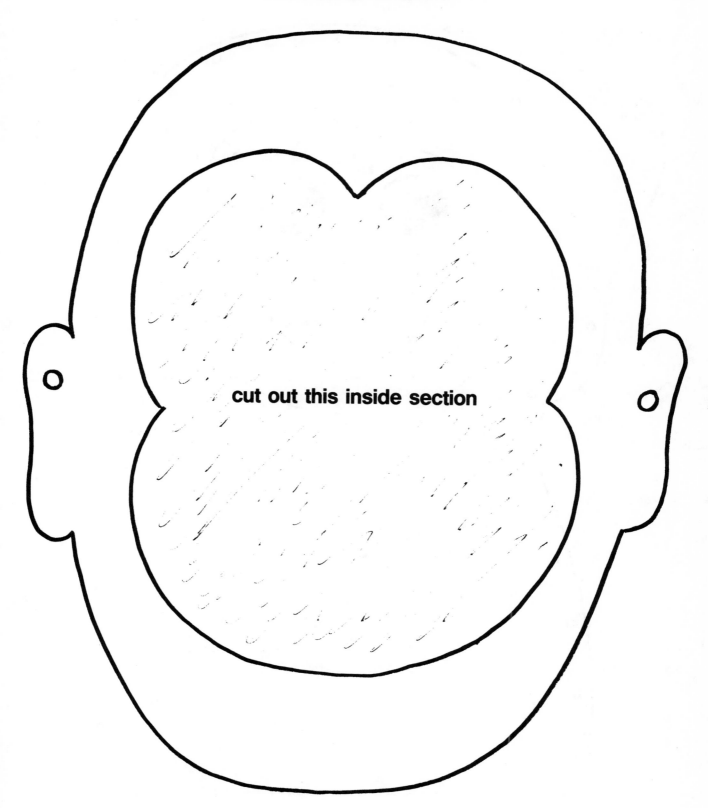

cut out this inside section

Monkey Hand Puppet

Monkey Under a Hat

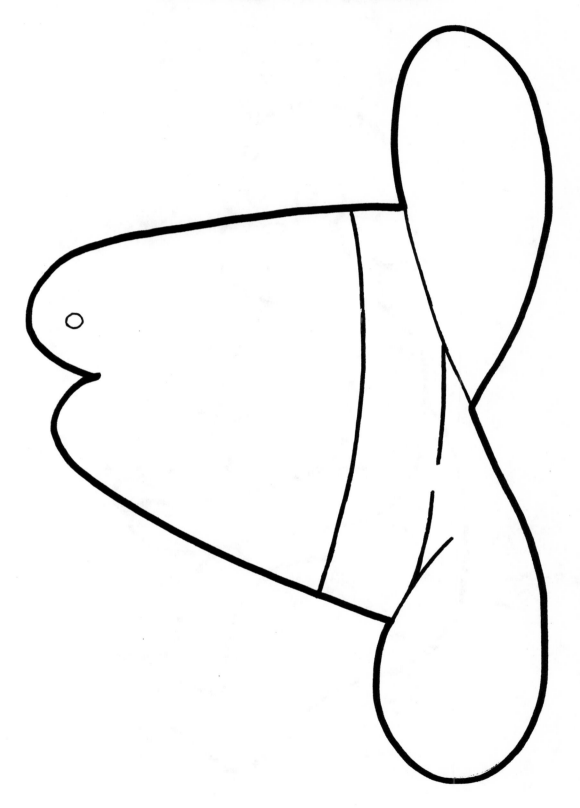

Monkey Under a Hat

Monkey and Balloons

Structured Story Starter:
Curious George

My curious animal is a _____

He lives with _____

He used to live in _____

But now he lives in _____

Here is what happened to him because he was curious:

_____

_____

_____

_____

_____

_____

_____

_____

Story Map: *Curious George*

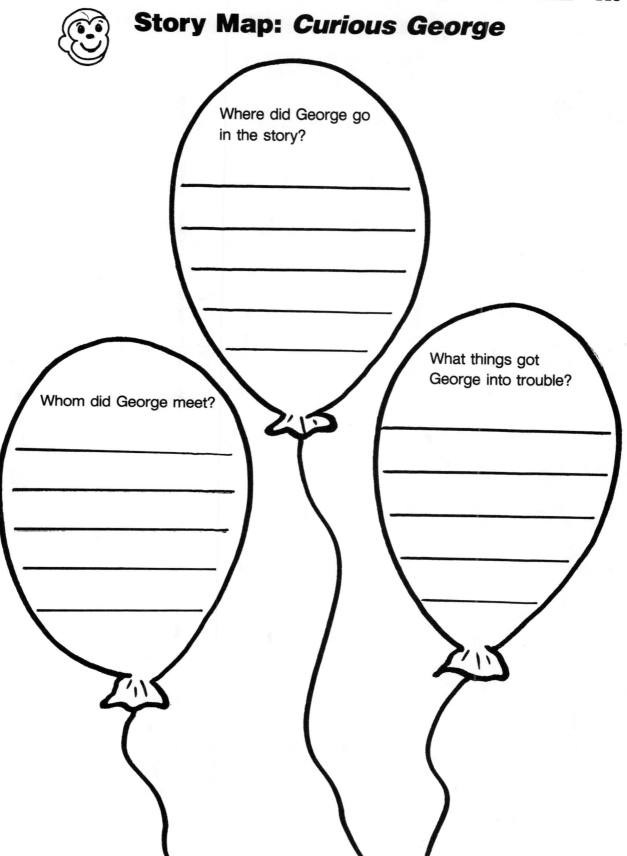

Where did George go
in the story?

_____

_____

_____

_____

Whom did George meet?

_____

_____

_____

_____

What things got
George into trouble?

_____

_____

_____

_____

116

Name _____

Help the Monkey

Help the monkey find the hat, telephone, and balloons.

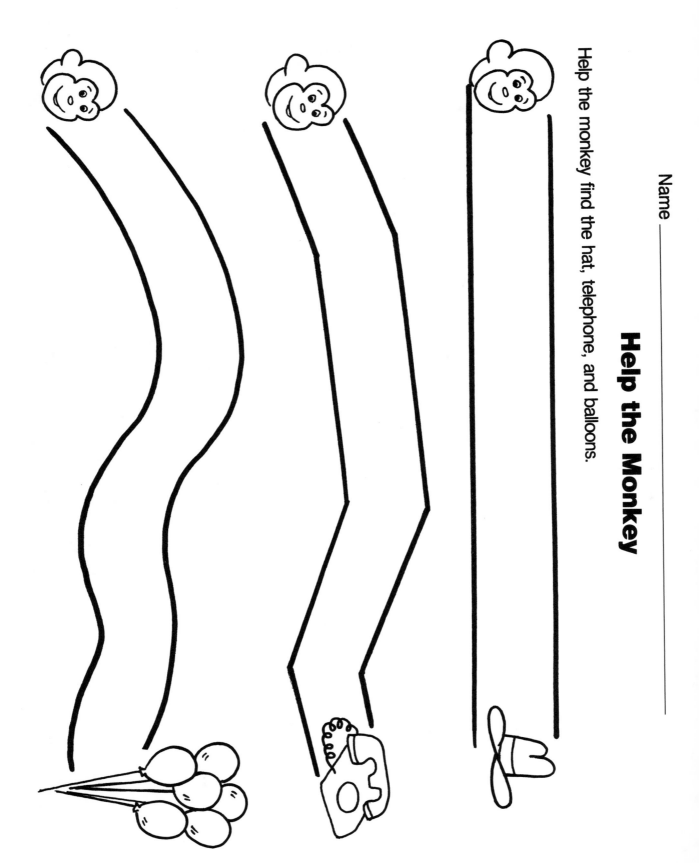

Monkey Maze

Help the monkey find the banana.

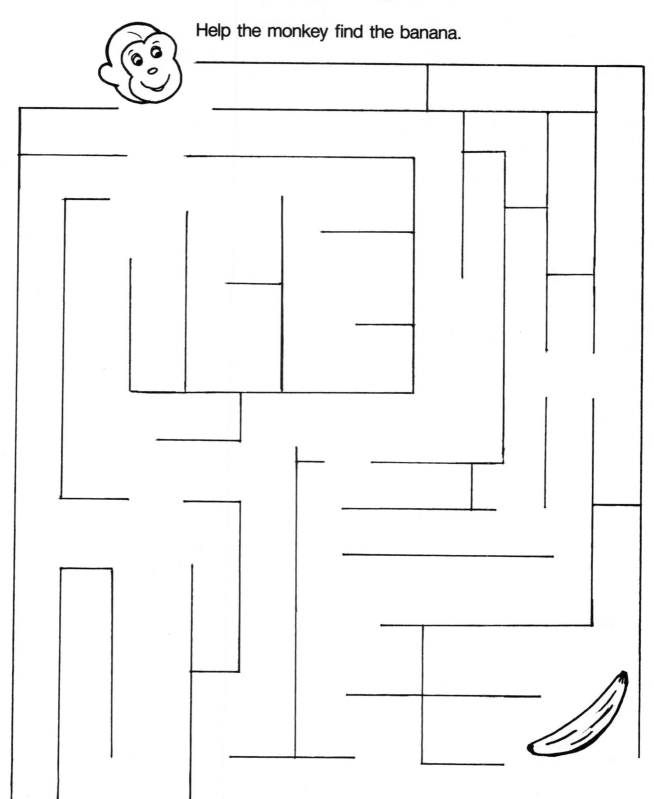

CHILDHOOD PROBLEMS

Tongue Depressor Baby
Peter's Chair

Bread and Jam
Bread and Jam for Frances

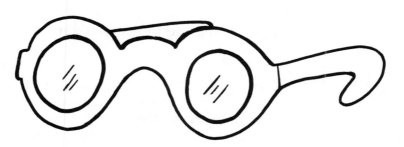

Eyeglasses
Arthur's Eyes

Arthur's Eyes, Marc Brown
Bread and Jam for Frances, Russell Hoban
Peter's Chair, Ezra Jack Keats

BEING DIFFERENT

Arthur's Eyes, Marc Brown, Little, Brown and Company, 1973.

Arthur needs eyeglasses. Will his friends make fun of him? Then, mysteriously, his eyeglasses keep disappearing.

Introductory Activity

Surprise Box   Put some old eyeglasses in the surprise box.

Art Activities

*Eyeglasses   Reproduce the eyeglass frame patterns on heavy tagboard. Let the children choose their favorite frame pattern, cut it out, and paint or color decorations. Show them how to use brass fasteners to attach the side pieces. The children will enjoy wearing their creations during class.

Apple Prints   Tell the children that they can use their eyes to see something exciting inside an apple. Then cut the apple across the core so the children can see a star! Let them dip apple halves in paint to make prints.

Painting   Encourage the children to create beautiful paintings or other artwork that pleases their eyes.

*Indicates activity that has an accompanying reproducible worksheet.

Wet Fun   Sprinkle several colors of dry tempera in a pan of water.
                     Lay a piece of paper on the water and swirl it around,
                     producing a pretty marbleized effect. This is an exciting art
                     experience to see.

Crayon Rubbings Here's another interesting visual effect. Lay a piece of
                     paper on various textured objects or tagboard cutouts and
                     rub over the paper with the side of a crayon. The children
                     find it exciting as they see a picture appear on the paper!

Language Development

Words to Grow By   headaches   frames
                       blind   photographer
                       optometrist

Something to   Why did Arthur need glasses?
Think About   Why didn't he want to wear glasses?
                       If Arthur didn't wear his glasses, what might happen if he
                           were watching a movie? crossing a street? playing
                           baseball?
                       Name some things that help us see more clearly.
                       Which one would you use to look at the stars?
                           see the chalkboard?
                           look at some grains of sand?
                           watch a movie?
                           look at a drop of water?
                           watch birds?
                           examine the bark of a tree?
                           look at a boat on the water?
                       Close your eyes. What do you see? Tell how your life would
                           be different if you couldn't see at all.

I See Something   Have each child pretend to wear glasses and describe
                       something she is looking at. The other children try to guess
                       what she is describing.

Indicates activity that has an accompanying reproducible worksheet.

Memory	Give the children a few minutes to study several objects on a tray. Then cover the tray and see how many objects they can name.
Detective	Have the children study one child carefully. Then place the child where the others can't see him and ask some questions—e. g., What color is his hair? Is he wearing a belt? Does he have a picture on his shirt?
*Hidden Animals	Challenge the children to use their sense of sight to find and circle the ten animals hidden in the drawing.
*Use Your Eyes	Allow older children to work individually or in teams to find and list the eight differences between the two pictures. Have younger children give their answers orally.
*Story Frame	Use the story frame to help children recall details and identify the main idea of a story. Not simply a fill-in-the-blanks activity, the story frame requires children to use their writing skills.

Fine and Gross Motor Skills _____

'Tis a Puzzlement	Emphasize to the children how valuable their eyes are as they work with puzzles, beads, pegs and pegboards.
Change Squares	Put carpet squares on the floor for all but two children. Tell the children that when you call out, "Change squares," they are to run to a different square. Children without squares try to get on squares. Repeat several times.
Beanbag Toss	Have the children take turns throwing beanbags in a basket or at a target.

Indicates activity that has an accompanying reproducible worksheet.

Musical Chairs Play this game several times just for the fun of it. With very young children, no one is ever "out." Emphasize to the children how valuable their eyes are when they play this game.

Fingerplays and Songs

As Eyes See It
by Mary Jane Butner and Janice Marks Sieplinga

What can you see with your eyes of blue?
In the bedroom, I see my daddy's big shoes.

What can you see with your eyes of brown?
In my toy box, I see a funny toy clown.

What can you see with your eyes of green?
In the basement, I see the washing machine.

There are so many wonderful things to be seen
With eyes that are blue, or brown or green!

Seeing, Seeing
by Jane Peterson
(Tune: "Sailing, Sailing")

Seeing, seeing.
I use my eyes to see.
They help me read a favorite book;
And sometimes watch TV.

Looking, looking,
Everywhere I go.
Using my eyes to help me learn
Everything I should know.

(Use the following verses with a unit on the senses.)

*Indicates activity that has an accompanying reproducible worksheet.

From *Learning Through Literature*, published by Scott, Foresman and Company.
Copyright © 1991 Mary Jane Butner, Jane Ann Peterson, and Janice Marks Sieplinga.

2. Hearing, hearing
   I use my ears to hear—
   A laugh, a cry, a friendly "Hi!"
   My ears bring sounds in clear.

   Listening, listening,
   Everywhere I go.
   Using my ears to help me learn
   Everything I should know.

3. Smelling, smelling,
   I use my nose to smell—
   The fragrance of a lovely flower,
   A steak upon the grill.

   Sniffing, sniffing,
   Everywhere I go.
   Using my nose to help me smell;
   Learning what pleases me so.

4. Tasting, tasting,
   I use my tongue to taste—
   Salty, sour, bitter, sweet,
   Just a lick and I know how it tastes.

   Savoring flavoring,
   Everywhere I go.
   Using my tongue to help me taste
   Learning what pleases me so.

5. Touching, touching,
   I use my hands to touch—
   Things that are bumpy, smooth, or soft;
   Things that are hard or rough.

   Reaching, feeling,
   Everywhere I go.
   Using my hands to help me learn
   Everything I should know.

Indicates activity that has an accompanying reproducible worksheet.

Color Find
by Jane Peterson and Janice Marks Sieplinga
(Tune: "Muffin Man")

Oh, (Matt), can you find something (red)?
Find something (red), find something (red)?
Oh, (Matt), can you find something (red)?
It's hiding in our room.

Oh, yes, I found something (red) , . . .
I think it is _____.

*(Continue this singing game until a child finds the item you are
thinking of. Use it with other colors.)*

Cooking

From This to That   Make butter, applesauce, scrambled eggs, or something else
that allows the children to see a change taking place in the
food being prepared.

Science

Vision Boosters   Put out a variety of "things that help us see": binoculars,
telescope, microscope, magnifying glasses, etc.

Math

Picture Graph   Prepare a large graph with headings that correspond to eye
colors. Have the children draw self-portraits on small paper
plates, being careful to make their eyes the right color.
Then have the children place their drawings under the
appropriate color heading, count the number of plates in
each category, and compare.

*Indicates activity that has an accompanying reproducible worksheet.

Extended Experiences

Field Trip   Arrange for a trip to an optical service where the children can try on eyeglass frames and see the equipment used for vision testing.

Resource Person   Invite an opthalmologist, optometrist, or optician to visit the class.

Related Books

The children will enjoy these other Arthur books by Marc Brown: *Arthur's Nose, Arthur's Tooth, Arthur's Valentine.*

Goggles, Ezra Jack Keats, The MacMillan Company, 1969.
  Peter and Archie outwit the big boys who want to take the goggles that Peter found.

---

*Indicates activity that has an accompanying reproducible worksheet.

Eyeglasses

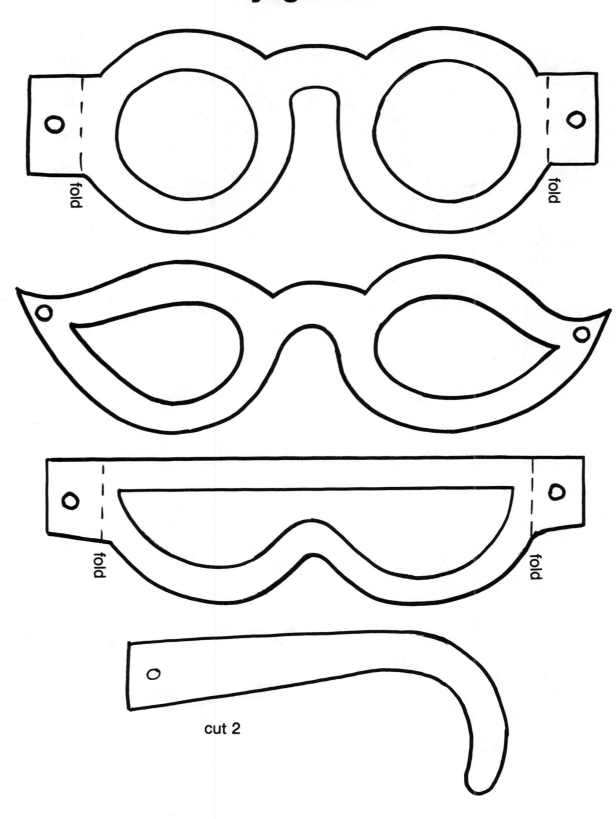

fold

fold

fold

fold

cut 2

Hidden Animals

Find the:
bird
chipmunk
deer
fish
rabbit
snail
snake
squirrel
turtle
worm

Name _____

Use Your Eyes

Can you find eight differences between the two pictures?

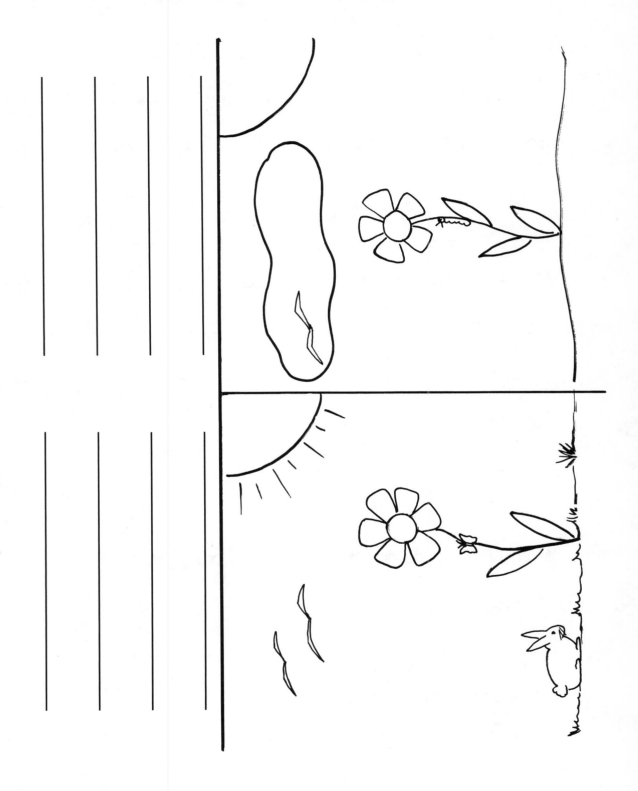

Story Frame: *Arthur's Eyes*

At the beginning of the story, Arthur had problems at school because

_____

_____

So his parents _____

_____

_____

After Arthur got glasses, his friends _____

_____

_____

This made Arthur _____

_____

_____

When Arthur found out that his teacher wore glasses, he _____

_____

_____

At the end of the story, Arthur learned that _____

_____

_____

FUSSY EATERS

Bread and Jam for Frances, Russell Hoban, Scholastic Book Services, 1974.

Frances will eat only bread and jam. Mother doesn't scold or lecture, but by the end of the story Frances is begging to try new foods. This story can serve as a good introduction to a lesson on nutrition.

Introductory Activity

Surprise Box   Put a slice of bread, a jar of jam, or a jump rope in the surprise box.

Art Activities

*Bread and Jam   Trace the pattern on light brown construction paper, and then have the children cut out the bread and staple it to a small paper plate. Let the children spread pudding or gelatin as they pretend to put jam on the bread.

For pudding painting, mix a small box of *instant* vanilla pudding with one cup of water. Add red food coloring. Let the children fingerpaint the mixture onto the bread.

For gelatin painting, gradually add a small amount of water to a package of raspberry or strawberry gelatin. The mixture should be fairly thick. The children can apply it with a paintbrush or spread it with a plastic knife.

*Indicates activity that has an accompanying reproducible worksheet.

My Favorite Dinner   Have the children cut out pictures of their favorite dinner foods from old newspapers and magazines. You may want to have the children bring pre-cut pictures from home. Encourage the children to choose one item from each of the four food groups and glue the four pictures to a large paper plate. For a more elaborate project, you can have the children mount their plates on 12x18-inch construction paper "placemats" and add utensils, a napkin, and a paper cup.

Language Development _____

Words to Grow By   badger   balance
                         poached   variety
                         nutrition   food groups
                         nutritious

Something to Think About

What is Frances's favorite food?
What foods do we need every day?
Can you explain why Frances was crying at dinner when she was given bread and jam?
Plan three good meals—breakfast, lunch, and dinner.
List the foods Frances's mother fixed, placing them in their proper food groups. Pretend you are talking to Frances, convincing her to try new foods.
Why do you think Frances's parents let her eat bread and jam for so many meals?

Let's Go Shopping   Collect a large assortment of food boxes and cans. Have the children make associations—e. g., something good for breakfast . . . a dessert treat . . . something you eat with a spoon . . . something you may have to cut with a knife, etc. By associating the product with the label, the children participate in a reading readiness activity.

*Indicates activity that has an accompanying reproducible worksheet.

From *Learning Through Literature*, published by Scott, Foresman and Company.
Copyright © 1991 Mary Jane Butner, Jane Ann Peterson, and Janice Marks Sieplinga.

The Alike Game

Using the food packages from "Let's Go Shopping," have a child pick two and tell how they are alike. There are many ways to classify food; they could be the same color, belong to the same food group, be stored in the same way, etc.

*Fruit, Meat, Vegetable?

You can do this activity as a group or an individual project. If you do it as an individual project, reproduce the two worksheet pages for each child. Tell the children to cut apart the food drawings and then paste each one under the correct heading for its food group.

Where Does It Come From?

Show the children pictures of various foods and ask where each food comes from. That's right, they all *do* come from the store! But before that . . . .

Dramatic Play

Supply the housekeeping center with pots, pans, dishes, food boxes and cans, aprons, and tablecloths for dramatic play.

*Story Frame

In addition to helping the children recall details of the story, this activity is valuable in helping them organize their thoughts and develop writing skills.

Fine and Gross Motor Skills

*Breakfast for Frances

Make a copy of the worksheet for each child. Tell the children to cut out the pictures and put them in the correct order to show how to make eggs for Frances. When they have the pictures in the correct order, the children can paste the pictures in the numbered boxes.

*Indicates activity that has an accompanying reproducible worksheet.

From *Learning Through Literature*, published by Scott, Foresman and Company. Copyright © 1991 Mary Jane Butner, Jane Ann Peterson, and Janice Marks Sieplinga.

Jumping Rope

Since Frances likes to jump rope, doing some rope activities with the children would be appropriate. Young children can pretend to swing the rope and jump over it; older children can do some actual rope jumping. Here are some other ideas for jumping rope:

> *Snake:* Make a rope wiggle along the ground. Tell the children they must jump over without stepping on the snake.
> *High and Low:* Have the children jump over the rope at various heights.
> *Rope Swing:* Have the children jump over the rope as you make it swing slightly.

Good Foods

Make a large circle on the floor. Inside the circle place food pictures (or actual food boxes and cans). Be sure to have both nutritious foods and sugary snacks represented, with at least one nutritious food for every child. Have the children move around the circle in time to music. When the music stops, each child must pick up a picture, box, or can representing a nutritious food.

Walk for Nutrition

This activity combines balance skills with a nutrition review. Have a tray of various foods—e. g., apple, cookies, candy bar, grapes, carrot, lettuce and radish, crackers, wrapped cheese slice, lollipop—in plastic sandwich bags. Ask each child to choose a nutritious food from the selections on the tray and then to carry it across the balance beam. Next, ask each child to choose a sugary food and carry it across the balance beam. Finally, have each child choose one nutritious food and one sugary food, carry both across the balance beam, and then explain why the nutritious food is good for you and the sugary food is not good for you.

*Breakfast Shadow Match

Make a copy of the worksheet for each child. In this visual discrimination activity, the children draw lines to match each food picture with its shadow.

---

*Indicates activity that has an accompanying reproducible worksheet.

Fingerplays and Songs _____

Food for Thought
by Mary Jane Butner and Jane Peterson

It's breakfast time, breakfast time.
Start the day right
With fruit juice and cereal,
And milk that is white.

It's lunchtime, it's lunchtime.
Oh what can we eat?
There's soup, cheese, and crackers,
A sandwich with meat.

It's dinnertime, dinnertime.
What's in the pan?
Green beans, and carrots,
And honey-baked ham.

But I am still hungry.
May I have a treat? Choose something nutritious—
Nothing too sweet.

(The children may also enjoy chanting "Jam on biscuits . . ." on page 10 of the story.)

Did You Ever Eat?
by Mary Jane Butner
(Tune: "Did You Ever See a Lassie?")

Did you ever eat poached eggs?
Eat poached eggs? Eat poached eggs?
Did you ever eat poached eggs,
And did they taste good?

Oh yes, they were yummy.
They tickled my tummy!
I have eaten poached eggs;
And yes, they were good!

(You can make up additional verses using other foods from the story—e. g., veal cutlets, string beans, spaghetti—or foods suggested by the children.)

*Indicates activity that has an accompanying reproducible worksheet.

Cooking

Bread and Jam for Us
Have the children make their own snack by spreading jam on bread.

Tasting Party
Have each child bring small samples of her favorite nutritious snack to share with the rest of the class.

Science

Veggie Investigation
Bring either some real vegetables or good pictures of vegetables to class. Discuss which part of the plant we eat—roots, leaves, stems, flowers, seeds.

Scientific Tasting
Have a tasting party to acquaint the children with different tastes (salty, sweet, sour, bitter, spicy, and bland). You can also discuss texture (hard, soft, crispy, dry, juicy) as well as smell and appearance.

Math

Set the Table
Put some plates on a table. Have the children put out a corresponding number of knives, forks, spoons, and napkins.

Food Graph

Make a graph based on three foods from the same food group—e. g., three fruits or three meats. Have each child choose his favorite of the three and mark the chart accordingly. Then have the children add the markings for each food and make comparisons among the three totals so as to find the favorite and least favorite.

Indicates activity that has an accompanying reproducible worksheet.

Extended Experiences

Field Trips   Take the children to visit a food processing plant or for a tour of a restaurant kitchen.

Resource Person   Invite a dietician to visit the class and discuss nutritious eating.

Related Books

Green Eggs and Ham, Dr. Seuss (Theodore Geisel), Random House, 1960.
> Who doesn't like green eggs and ham? Only someone who hasn't tried this delectable treat!

Mexicali Soup, Kathryn Hitte, Parent's Magazine Press, 1970.
> Everyone loves Mama's soup, but everyone has a suggestion for one ingredient that should be left out. Pretty soon there's nothing left but hot water!

Frances is a very "human" badger. She has trouble with her friends, is jealous of her sister, and doesn't like to go to bed. Mother and Father use their gentle, humorous problem-solving skills to help her. The children will enjoy these other Frances books by Russell Hoban:
Best Friends for Frances, Bedtime for Frances, A Bargain for Frances, A Baby Sister for Frances, A Birthday for Frances.

---

*Indicates activity that has an accompanying reproducible worksheet.

Bread and Jam

Fruit, Meat, Vegetable?

Name

Fruit, Meat, Vegetable?

Dairy Products	Meats	Fruits and Vegetables	Breads and Cereals

Story Frame:
Bread and Jam for Frances

The problem in this story is _____

_____

_____

At the beginning of the story, Father, Mother, and Gloria are

_____

Frances is _____

_____

For lunch Frances has _____

_____

For dinner she has _____

_____

So the next day, Mother gives Frances _____

_____

At dinner, Frances starts to cry because _____

_____

The problem is solved when Frances learns _____

_____

Name _____

cut on dotted line

1.

2.

3.

Breakfast for Frances

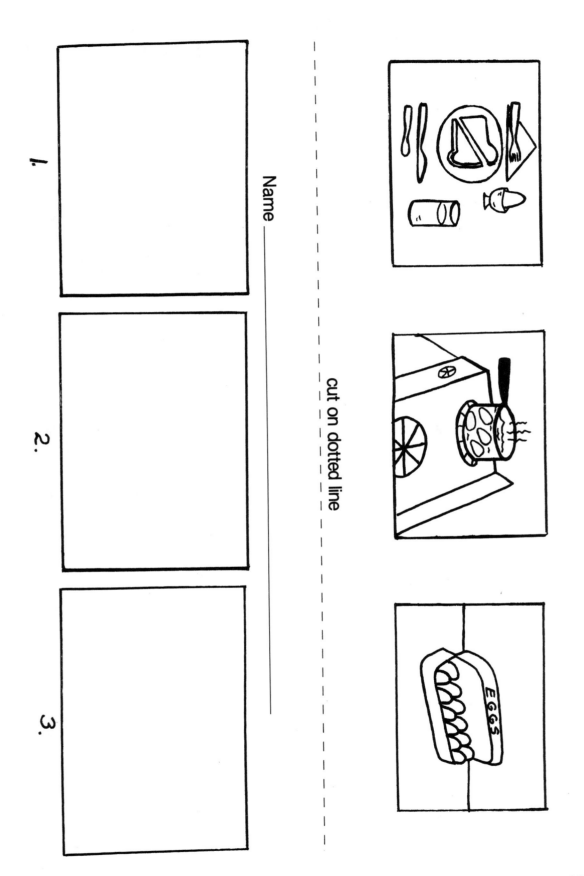

EGGS

Breakfast Shadow Match

FAMILY RELATIONSHIPS

Peter's Chair, Ezra Jack Keats, Harper and Row, 1967.
Everything is being painted pink at Peter's house—*his* cradle, *his* high chair, *his* crib—all for the new baby. Maybe he can save his chair.

Introductory Activity

Surprise Box   Place a baby item—baby shoes, baby bottle, feeding spoon, etc.—in the surprise box.

Art Activities

*Baby and Cradle   Each child can make a baby by adding facial features and a wisp of cotton hair to half of a large tongue depressor or a wooden ice cream spoon. Glue a cotton ball to the lower spoon area for baby's tummy. A 4-inch square of flannel makes a baby blanket, which can be glued in place or held together with a small gold safety pin. The children can make cradles by following the guidelines on the worksheet pattern.

Pink Painting   Let the children mix red and white paint together to discover that they can make pink. Then let them paint pink pictures.

Pink Collage   Put out pink yarn, ribbon, lace, buttons, wallpaper samples, etc. The children can glue the items on a cradle, rattle, or baby bootie cutout to make pink collages.

---

*Indicates activity that has an accompanying reproducible worksheet.

*Trace and Color Peter's Chair

Instruct the children to trace the broken lines and then to color and decorate Peter's chair.

Mobile

Tell the children that this activity gives them a chance to make a gift for a real baby. Explain that babies like to look at large bright objects. Let the children cut out three large shapes from brightly colored paper and attach the shapes with strings to a clothes hanger or wooden dowel. You may want to include a warning with the gift that it should be kept out of baby's reach.

*Stuffed Toys

Have the children select their favorite pattern: ball, rabbit, or cat. Then lay it on material and cut out two pieces. Pin the pieces right sides together, and sew around (leaving a ¼-inch seam allowance) using a short running stitch. Leave an opening at the bottom to allow for stuffing. Clip curves and turn. Fill with polyfiber filler or clean nylon stockings. When the toy is filled, slip stitch the opening. Facial features may be sewn on, but if the toy is to be given to a young child, draw the features with fabric markers.

Language Development

Words to Grow By

While the vocabulary in *Peter's Chair* is minimal, you may want to introduce some of the following words when discussing the story:

    outgrow   jealousy
    jealous

Something to Think About

Do you have a baby brother or sister?
Have you ever had to give up something to a younger brother or sister?
In the story, what color is everything being painted?
Why is Peter unhappy?
What changes occur when a new baby is in the house?
How have Peter's feelings changed by the end of the story?

---

*Indicates activity that has an accompanying reproducible worksheet.

From *Learning Through Literature*, published by Scott, Foresman and Company.
Copyright © 1991 Mary Jane Butner, Jane Ann Peterson, and Janice Marks Sieplinga.

Who's Who?   Have the children bring in baby pictures as well as recent
                        pictures of themselves. Have them try to guess the
                        identities of the babies. Then compare each baby picture
                        with a recent picture, and talk about how the children
                        have changed.

Babies and Big   Have the children make lists of things they can do now
Kids   that they couldn't do as babies.

*Story Frame   Use the story frame to help the children recall details and
                        identify main ideas in the story.

Fine and Gross Motor Skills ───────────────

*Who Would   Make a copy of the two worksheet pages for each child.
Use It?   Have the children cut out the pictures and glue them in the
                        appropriate columns, classifying each picture by whether it
                        is used by a baby or a bigger child.

Big Kid Fun—   As the children lace cards, string beads, work puzzles, or
Fine Motor   put pegs into pegboards, tell them that these things are too
                        difficult for babies to do.

Big Kid Fun—   Have the children bounce balls, throw and catch beanbags,
Gross Motor   walk across the balance beam, or run through an obstacle
                        course. Then congratulate the children on being able to do
                        things that babies can't do!

───

*Indicates activity that has an accompanying reproducible worksheet.

Fingerplays and Songs

Baby

by Mary Jane Butner, Jane Peterson, and
Janice Marks Sieplinga

See my baby, tiny baby,
In his cradle bed.
Wrap him warmly
In his blanket
Kiss him on the head.

See my baby, tiny baby,
In his cradle deep.
Rock him gently
Back and forth,
Until he's fast asleep.

'Cause I'm Big

by Jane Peterson
(Tune: "Polly Wolly Doodle")

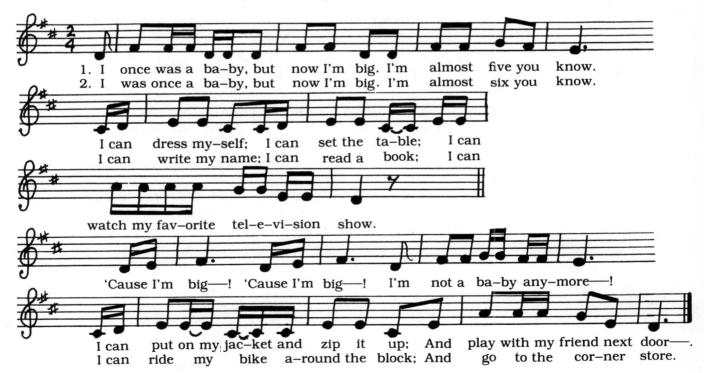

1. I once was a ba–by, but now I'm big. I'm almost five you know.
2. I was once a ba–by, but now I'm big. I'm almost six you know.

I can dress my–self; I can set the ta–ble; I can
I can write my name; I can read a book; I can

watch my fav–orite tel–e–vi–sion show.

'Cause I'm big——! 'Cause I'm big——! I'm not a ba–by any–more——!

I can put on my jac–ket and zip it up; And play with my friend next door——.
I can ride my bike a–round the block; And go to the cor–ner store.

Indicates activity that has an accompanying reproducible worksheet.

Traditional   *Rock-a-Bye, Baby*
                         Bye Baby Bunting

Cooking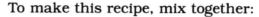

Applesauce   Ask each child to bring an apple. Then have all the
                        children help peel and slice the apples, add sugar and
    cinnamon, and stir over a hotplate to make applesauce.
                        Emphasize that *older* children can help with cooking while
                        babies cannot. As an extra activity, bring in a jar of
                        commercial applesauce and let the children compare it
                        with the applesauce that they made and describe how the
                        two differ.

Carrot Bars   To make this recipe, mix together:

    2 eggs (well beaten)   1 cup sugar
                        6 Tbsp. salad oil   1 cup flour
                        1 tsp. baking soda   ½ tsp. salt
                        1 tsp. cinnamon   1 jar junior carrots (baby
                                                         food)

                        Pour the batter into a 9x13-inch pan. Bake at 350° for 20-
                        30 minutes.

                        To make frosting for the carrot bars, mix together:
                        2 Tbsp. soft margarine   1 3-oz. package of cream
                        ¼ tsp. vanilla   cheese
                                                      ½ box powdered sugar

                        Point out to the children that while this recipe uses baby
                        food, they are able to make the frosted carrot bars (and
                        other simple recipes) because they are no longer babies.

Indicates activity that has an accompanying reproducible worksheet.

Science

Growth and Development

Check your library for good books that introduce young children to the details of prenatal development, birth, and postnatal growth and development. You may want to examine the books carefully regarding the amount of explicit or graphic detail, and then bring those books into the classroom that are acceptable to you, your students, the children's parents, and the school administration.

Math

Then and Now Chart

NAME	BORN	NOW
Aimee	6 lb. 10 oz. 19"	92 lbs. 4'8"
Jonathan	7 lb. 13 oz. 21½"	115 lbs. 5'11"
Andrew	7 lb. 11 oz. 20"	105 lbs. 5'6"
Dale		
Matt B.		
Ed		

Have the children bring in information regarding their birth weight and length. Then weigh and measure each child. Make a chart comparing the children as they are now to what they were as newborns.

Size Comparisons

Bring in a pair of baby shoes and have the children compare the shoes with the ones they are wearing now.

Seriation

Bring in actual items of clothing—shoes, shirts, hats, etc.—in infant, child, and adult sizes. Have the children arrange the clothing from smallest to largest.

Indicates activity that has an accompanying reproducible worksheet.

Extended Experiences

Field Trips
If your group is small enough, consider taking the children to visit a baby at someone's home. Be sure to point out all of the equipment that is needed to care for a baby. You could also take a trip to a department store to look at the baby clothes and furniture.

Resource Person
Invite a parent with a new baby to bring the infant to class, along with a diaper bag, bottle, and stroller or infant carrier.

Related Books

Big or Little, Kathy Stinson, Annick Press, Toronto, 1983.
When you're four years old, there are times when you feel very big—and times when you still feel very little.

A Baby Sister for Frances, Russell Hoban, Harper and Row, 1964.
The service isn't so good at Frances's house since Gloria's arrival. Time to run away!

Big Brother, Robert Kraus, Parents' Magazine Press, 1973.
Little Rabbit will always be smaller and younger than his big brother. Then Mother Rabbit brings a surprise home from the hospital. Now Little Rabbit is a big brother too!

She Come Bringing Me That Little Baby Girl, Eloise Greenfield, J. B. Lippincott Company, 1974.
At first, Kevin isn't happy to have a little sister. But a baby girl can quickly work her way into a big brother's heart!

All of these books provide factual information about human growth and development:
It's a Baby, George Arcona, E. P. Dutton, 1979.
Making Babies, Sara Bonnett Stein, Walker and Company, 1974.
That New Baby, Sara Bonnett Stein, Walker and Company, 1974.
The New Baby, Fred Rogers, G. P. Putnam's Sons, 1985.

*Indicates activity that has an accompanying reproducible worksheet.

Baby and Cradle

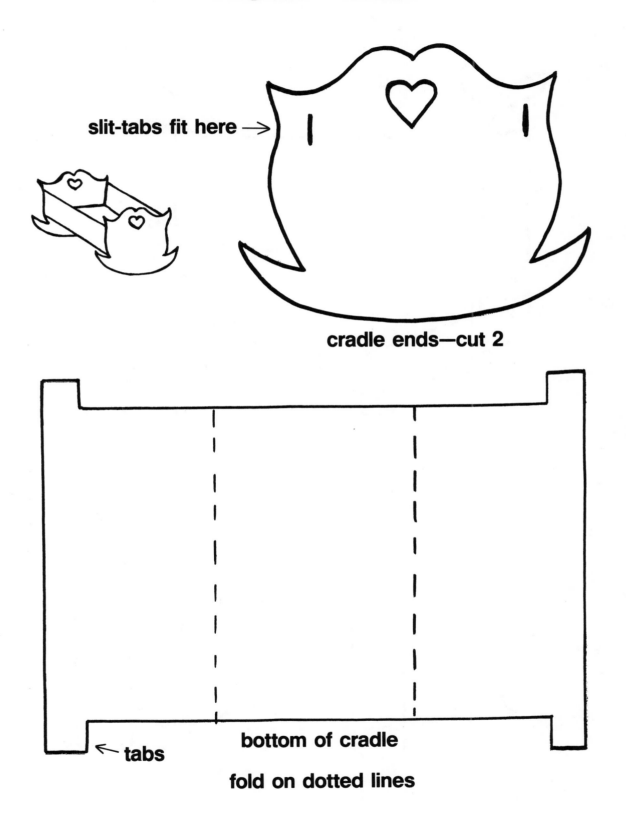

slit-tabs fit here →

cradle ends—cut 2

← tabs

bottom of cradle

fold on dotted lines

Trace and Color Peter's Chair

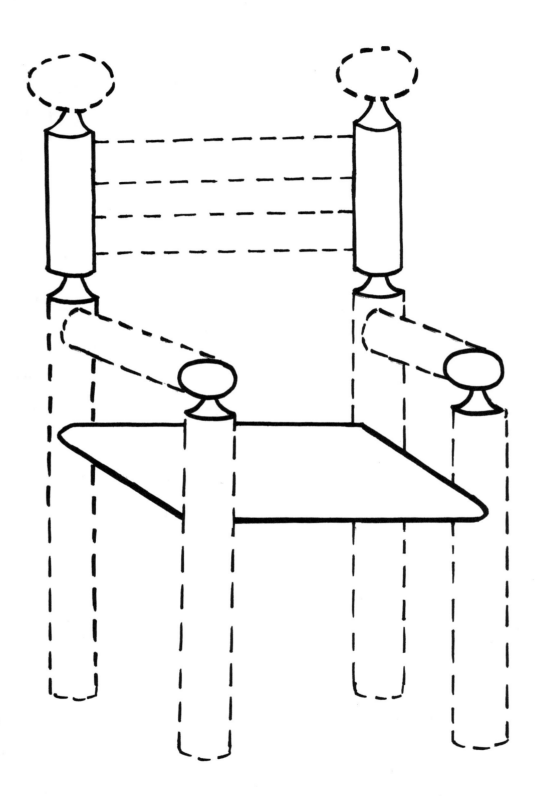

Stuffed Toys

ball pattern

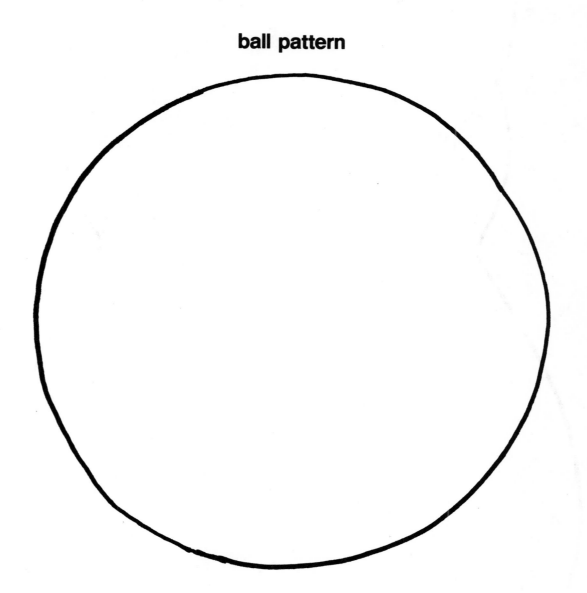

Stuffed Toys

cat pattern

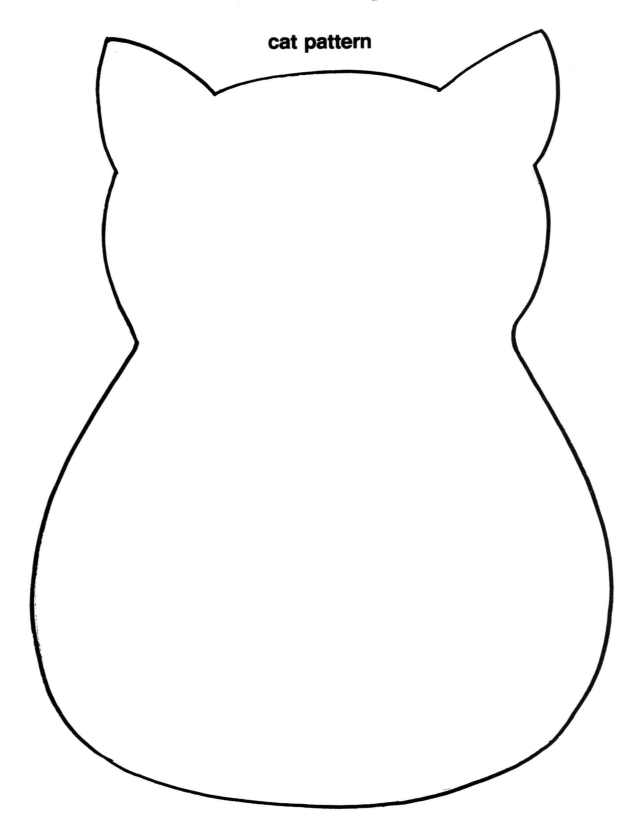

Stuffed Toys

bunny pattern

Story Frame: *Peter's Chair*

The problem in this story is _____

_____

Because of the new baby, Peter can't _____

_____

Because of the new baby, Peter's mother and father are _____

_____

_____

So Peter decides to _____

_____

He takes _____

_____

The problem is solved when Peter learns _____

_____

_____

At the end of the story, Peter _____

_____

_____

Who Would Use It?

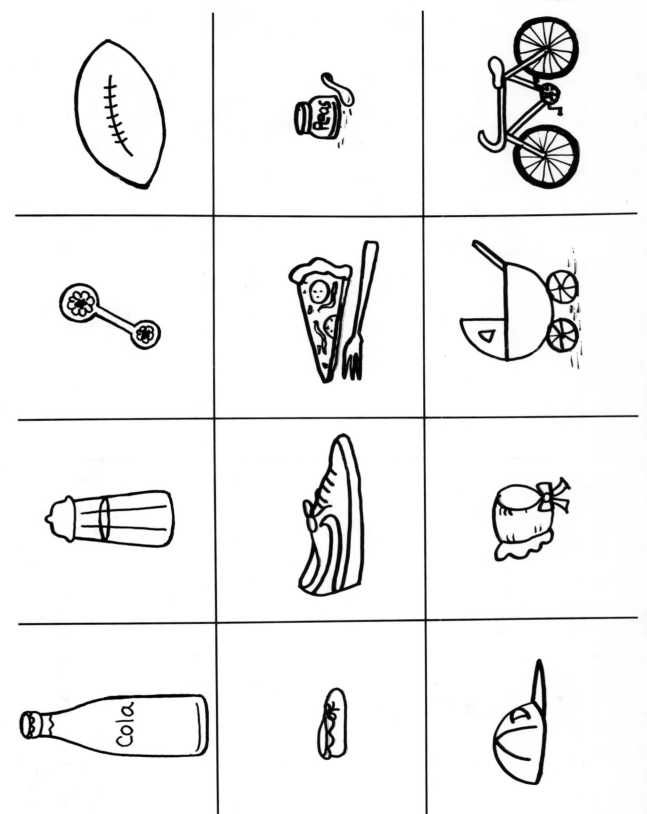

Name _____

Who Would Use It?

Baby

Big Girl or Boy

COMMUNITY HELPERS

Brush Your Teeth
Doctor DeSoto

Firefighting Bear
The Great Big Fire Engine Book

Fire Truck
The Great Big Fire Engine Book

Doctor DeSoto, William Steig
The Great Big Fire Engine Book

DENTIST

Doctor DeSoto, William Steig, Farrar, Straus and Giroux, 1982.
How does a mouse dentist deal with a patient who wants to eat him? Doctor DeSoto solves his problem in a humorous and diabolically clever fashion. A Newberry Honor Book.

Introductory Activities

Surprise Box

Put a tooth, toothbrush, or dental tool in the surprise box.

*Flannelboard Visual Aids

Use the patterns to make flannelboard cutouts of a toothbrush, toothpaste tube, floss, a happy tooth, and a sad tooth. You may want to use these flannelboard cutouts as part of your introduction to a unit on dental health.

Art Activities

*Giant Toothbrush and Toothpaste

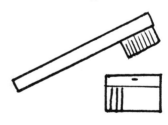

To make the toothbrush handle, fold a 6x18-inch sheet of construction paper so that it measures 1½x18 inches. To add the bristles, staple four pieces of 4x6-inch white paper between the folds near one end. Then staple all along the handle. Have the children fringe the bristles. You may want to print on the handle (or have the children print): "Brush your teeth."

Combine the two parts of the toothpaste tube to make one pattern which can be reproduced on 8½x14-inch paper. You may want to reproduce the cap and label on colored construction paper. The children then cut out all the parts and paste them together. As they work, they may want to talk about the brand of toothpaste they use. If so, let them print the brand name on the label.

*Indicates activity that has an accompanying reproducible worksheet.

**Good Foods/
Bad Foods—1**

Cut two large teeth out of posterboard—a smiling tooth and a frowning tooth with cavities. Have the children bring pictures from home showing foods that are good for healthy teeth and foods that are bad, and then have them paste their pictures on the appropriate tooth. You can then post the teeth collages on a dental health bulletin board.

***Good Foods/
Bad Foods—2**

Make two copies per child of the #1 size pattern from the "Tooth Patterns" worksheet. Have the children make one a happy tooth and the other a sad tooth. Then give each child a copy of the "Good Foods/Bad Foods" worksheet. Have the children color all the pictures, cut out the squares, and then paste the nutritious foods on the happy tooth and the sugary foods on the sad tooth.

*Tooth Puppets

Have the children cut out two of the #3 size tooth pattern. Tell them to make one a happy tooth and the other a sad tooth. Tape the teeth to craft sticks or to plastic sandwich bags. Then show the children food pictures clipped from magazines and mounted on index cards. The children decide whether the foods are good or bad for their teeth and hold up either the happy or the sad tooth.

*Big Mouth

Reproduce the mouth on red paper for each child. They can add teeth by sponge painting or making potato prints. For sponge painting, the children will need sponges cut into small squares; it sometimes helps to wet the sponge before cutting it. Give each child a clip clothespin to use as a handle for dipping the sponge into white paint and then dabbing on the paper. For making potato prints, cut potatoes in half and then cut away from the exposed inner surface so that a raised square appears in the middle. The children dip this square in white paint and then press on the paper to make teeth.

---

*Indicates activity that has an accompanying reproducible worksheet.

*Brush Your Teeth!

Use the #2 pattern from the "Tooth Patterns" worksheet. Have the children cut out a tooth and draw a happy face on it. Then have them make a toothbrush, using a 1x9-inch strip of construction paper for the handle and a 2x3-inch piece for the bristles. The children then paste the toothbrush on the tooth.

*Spatter Painting

For this activity you will need an old window screen, old toothbrushes, and a plastic tub. Start by making cutouts of teeth, toothbrushes, and nutritious foods. Have each child choose several of the cutouts (which can be reused) and place them on a piece of construction paper in the tub. Put the screen over the tub. The child dips a toothbrush into thinned paint and rubs the bristles over the screen, spattering paint onto the construction paper around the cutouts. When the child finishes painting, remove the screen, lift up the cutouts, and let the artist admire the effect!

Language Development

Words to Grow By

Many young children may be unfamiliar with some of the words in *Doctor DeSoto*. Therefore, your dramatic reading of the story, your facial expressions, and your vocal inflections can provide the necessary clues to help the children expand their vocabularies.

Doctor DeSoto contains wonderfully descriptive verbs (e.g., hoisted, gasped, whimpered, quiver, yank, chortled, lugging) as well as strong adjectives and adverbs (e.g., bitterly, pitiful, woozy, shabby, wicked, stunned, clenched).

After the children have heard and enjoyed the story, you may want to do some activities that enrich and extend their vocabularies. For example, you might reread some of the sentences in the story to see if the children can discover word meanings from context. Or you might reread passages and ask the children to listen for certain words that might mean the same as cried (whimpered), pulling (lugging), or bad (wicked), etc. Try to make a point of using some of the words in conversation with the children during the school day.

---

*Indicates activity that has an accompanying reproducible worksheet.

From *Learning Through Literature*, published by Scott, Foresman and Company.
Copyright © 1991 Mary Jane Butner, Jane Ann Peterson, and Janice Marks Sieplinga.

Something to Think About

Who went to the dentist?

Why did he go?

If you were Doctor DeSoto, would you have let the fox in? Why or why not?

List ways Doctor DeSoto's office is like any dentist's office. How is his office different?

Think of another way Doctor DeSoto could have solved his problem with the fox.

What things in the story show that Doctor DeSoto and his wife were kind? brave? smart?

Chart Story

If you visit a dentist's office, record the children's ideas and experiences in a chart story.

Creative Dramatics

Have the children pretend that their teeth are glued together like the fox's. Or have them pretend to be Doctor DeSoto walking on the fox's tongue.

Healthy Teeth

Ask a child to say, "To keep my teeth healthy, I'm going to . . ." and then complete the sentence by adding "brush every day," "drink milk," "go to the dentist," etc. Then call on another child to repeat what the first one said and to add a new idea. Continue, with each succeeding child repeating the whole list before adding another idea. In a class of very young children, it might be wise to have the whole group repeat the list.

Category: Healthy Foods

This rhythmic game encourages classifying skills and quick thinking. Have the children sit on the floor in a circle. Everyone in sequence slaps knees, claps hands, and snaps fingers twice. While snapping fingers, each successive child must name an item that fits the category—in this case, healthy foods. Anyone who can't think of an item is out. This game may be difficult at first for younger children; but if you start slowly, they may be able to catch on.

Indicates activity that has an accompanying reproducible worksheet.

From *Learning Through Literature*, published by Scott, Foresman and Company.
Copyright © 1991 Mary Jane Butner, Jane Ann Peterson, and Janice Marks Sieplinga.

Toothbrush Match   Make a game that combines reading readiness, color matching, and dental health awareness. Make toothbrush handles out of 1x7 ½-inch strips of colored posterboard, and use 2-inch squares of white posterboard for the bristles. Make six to eight toothbrushes in *each* of these colors: red, orange, green, blue, yellow, and purple. Print the color word on each toothbrush. Make a set of cards labeled with the same color words. Lay out the cards and have the children place the correct toothbrush on each one by matching the letter patterns.

*Story Frame   In addition to helping children recall details and identify the main idea of a story, a story frame requires the use of writing skills. It is *not* simply a fill-in-the-blanks activity.

Fine and Gross Motor Skills

*Help the Teeth   As the children help the teeth down the paths, they gain both left-to-right readiness and dental health awareness.

*Munchy Misfits   Use this reproducible worksheet to help the children develop thinking and classifying skills while learning about the four food groups.

*Toothbrush Dot-to-Dot   While reinforcing the basic message of dental health, this activity helps children with number recognition.

*The Path to Healthy Teeth   The children will make decisions about good and bad foods as they develop tracking skills and fine motor control.

*Indicates activity that has an accompanying reproducible worksheet.

The Good Foods Walk

Prepare a tray of sample foods—e.g., apple, cookies, candy bar, grapes, carrot, lettuce and radish, crackers, cheese slice, lollipop, etc.—in small sandwich bags. Ask a child to choose one good nutritious food from the tray and carry it across the balance beam. Then ask the child to choose a food with lots of sugar (one that requires careful teeth brushing after eating) and carry it across the balance beam. Finally, ask the child to choose one nutritious food and one sugary food to carry across the balance beam. After this third trip across the balance beam, the child should explain which food is good for teeth and which one is bad.

Drop the Toothbrush

In this variation of "Duck, Duck, Goose," the child who is "it" drops a toothbrush behind the child who will chase her. The toothbrush acts as a marker so that the children know where to stop.

Pass the Toothbrush

Form the children into two or more teams, each standing in a straight line, with the children one behind the other. Each team has a set of different color toothbrushes (from "Toothbrush Match"). At a signal, the first person on each team passes one toothbrush over his head to the next person, who passes it on, and so on to the end of the line. The teams continue to pass toothbrushes—one at a time—until the complete set is at the back of the line.

Toothbrush Relay

Pile all the toothbrushes from "Toothbrush Match" at one end of the classroom or gym. Divide the class into teams and assign each team a color. Everyone on the team takes a turn running down, finding a toothbrush of the correct color, and returning to the relay line.

Indicates activity that has an accompanying reproducible worksheet.

Fingerplays and Songs _____

Your Teeth Are Important
by Mary Jane Butner, Jane Peterson, Janice Marks Sieplinga
(Tune: "Sweet Betsy from Pike")

Your teeth are important—they help you to chew;
They help you to smile and say "How do you do?"
Be sure to take care of them morning and night.
By brushing and flossing you'll keep your teeth bright.

**A Tooth Tale*
by Mary Jane Butner

Ten baby teeth chomping food so fine,
One fell out—then there were nine.
Nine baby teeth said, "Chewing is great!"
One fell out—then there were eight.
Eight baby teeth said, "We belong to Kevin."
Kevin bit an apple—then there were seven.
Seven baby teeth munching pretzel sticks,
One fell out—then there were six.
Six baby teeth gulping cottage cheese with chives,
One fell out—then there were five.
Five baby teeth cried, "We want to eat some more!"
One fell out—then there were four.
Four baby teeth said, "Is that a carrot stick we see?"
They bit into that carrot—then there were three.
Three baby teeth sobbed, "We bit off more than we can chew."
One fell out—then there were two.
Two baby teeth gnawed a hot cross bun,
One fell out—then there was one.
One baby tooth exclaimed, "I can hardly chew this crumb."
One fell out—and then there were none. BUT
All the time those baby teeth were falling one by one,
Some new teeth were growing in. And now my tooth tale's done.

** Accompanying reproducible worksheet provides mouth and teeth
patterns to make flanneboard cutouts for use with A Tooth Tale.*

_____

*Indicates activity that has an accompanying reproducible worksheet.

Keep on Brushing
by Jane Peterson
(Tune: "Caisson Song")

Up and down, round and round,
Brush your teeth to keep them sound.
Keep on smiling and brushing your teeth.
When you brush every day,
You are fighting tooth decay.
Keep on smiling and brushing your teeth.

The dentist is your friend—
One on whom you can depend;
Visit him reg-u-lar-ly.
And where'er you go,
Let your smile show.
Keep on smiling and brushing your teeth—
That's right, floss too!
Keep on brushing and flossing your teeth.

Cooking

Fruit Kabobs Put out bowls of good foods—apple and orange slices, grapes, cheese cubes, strawberries, melon balls—and let the children make their own fruit kabobs on toothpicks.

Science

Why Are Teeth Important? Ask the children some questions about teeth: Why do they need teeth? What problems would they experience if they didn't have teeth? Do they know any people who don't have teeth?

And Nothing But the Tooth Bring in some actual teeth for display. Some may be children's baby teeth (dropped by a careless "Tooth Fairy"), but also ask a veterinarian for animal teeth that the children could examine.

Indicates activity that has an accompanying reproducible worksheet.

Math

Graphs

Did you brush?	
YES	NO
Lori	Tim
Pat	Matt
Tammy	
Tom	

Ask one of the following questions and then graph the children's responses:

Did you brush your teeth today?

Have you ever gone to the dentist?

What kind of toothpaste do you use?

Extended Experiences

Field Trip

Take the children to visit a dentist's office.

Resource Person

Invite a dentist or dental hygienist to visit your classroom.

Keeping a Chart

Have the children keep a toothbrushing chart at home for one week. Award Happy Tooth stickers (available through school catalogs) to all children who return the completed chart to school.

Brush Your Teeth				
Mon.	Tues.	Wed.	Thurs.	Fri.
☺	☺			

Related Books

Arthur's Tooth, Marc Brown, The Atlantic Monthly Press, 1985.
  Arthur is embarrassed because he is the only one in his class
  who hasn't lost a tooth yet.
My Dentist, Harlow Rockwell, Mulberry Books, 1975.
Taryn Goes to the Dentist, Jill Krementz, Crown Publishers, 1986.
The Wobbly Tooth, Nancy Evans Cooney, G. P. Putnam's Sons, 1978.
Little Rabbit's Loose Tooth, Lucy Bate, Crown Publishers, 1975.

*Indicates activity that has an accompanying reproducible worksheet.

From *Learning Through Literature*, published by Scott, Foresman and Company.
Copyright © 1991 Mary Jane Butner, Jane Ann Peterson, and Janice Marks Sieplinga.

Flannelboard Visual Aids

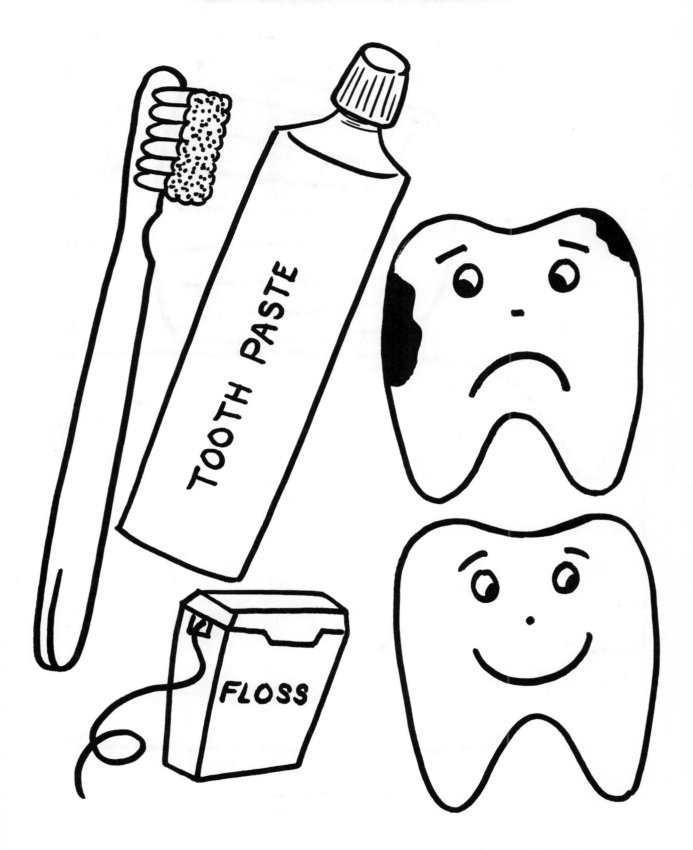

Giant Toothpaste Tube

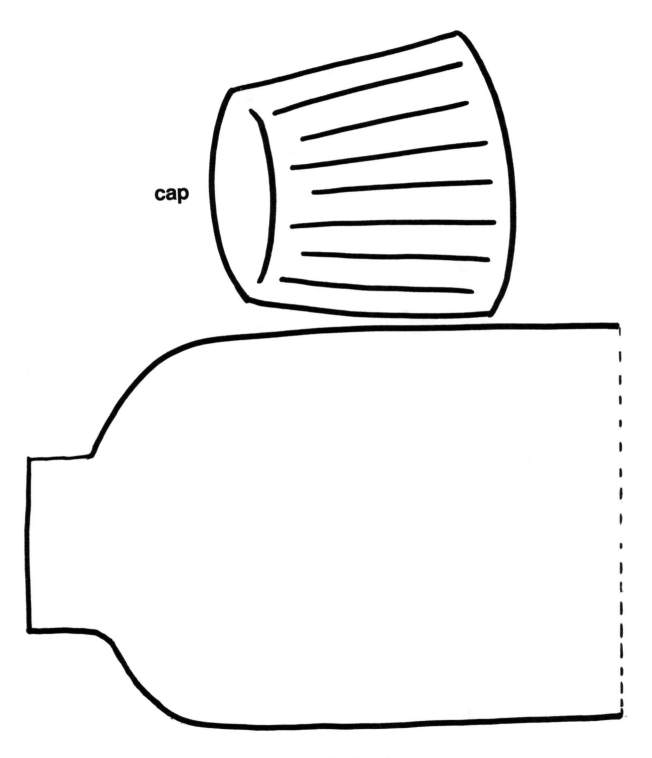

cap

top half of tube

Giant Toothpaste Tube

label

Toothpaste

bottom of tube

Good Foods/Bad Foods

Tooth Patterns

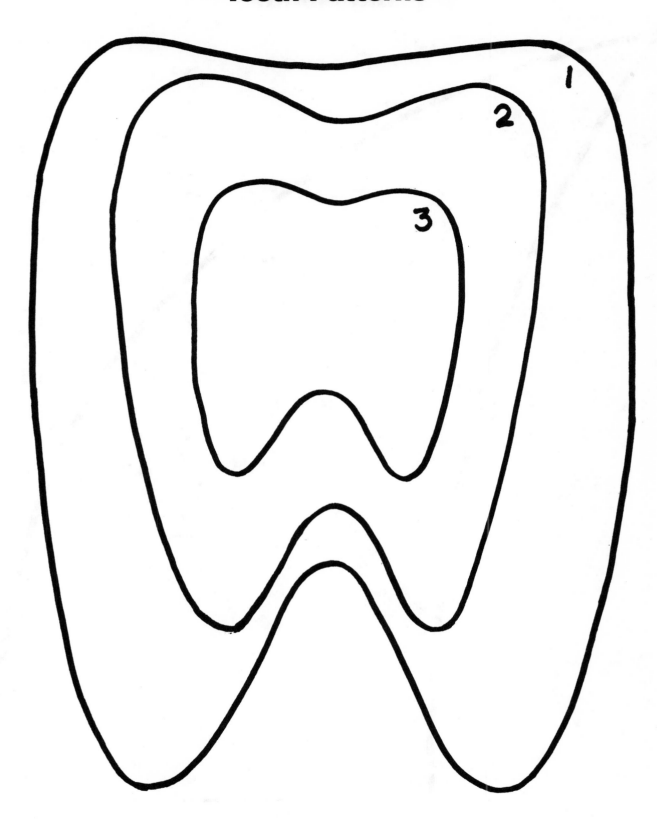

Big Mouth

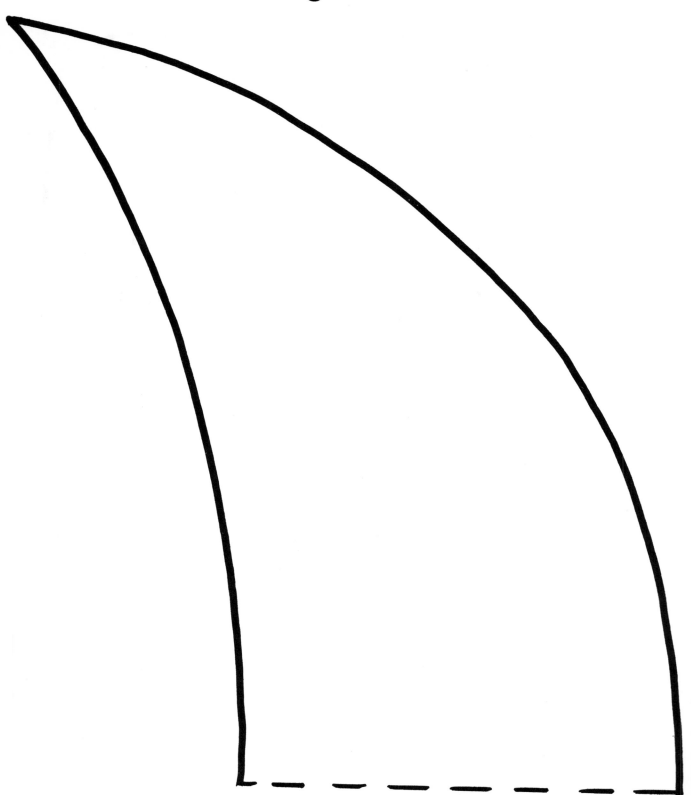

Spatter Painting

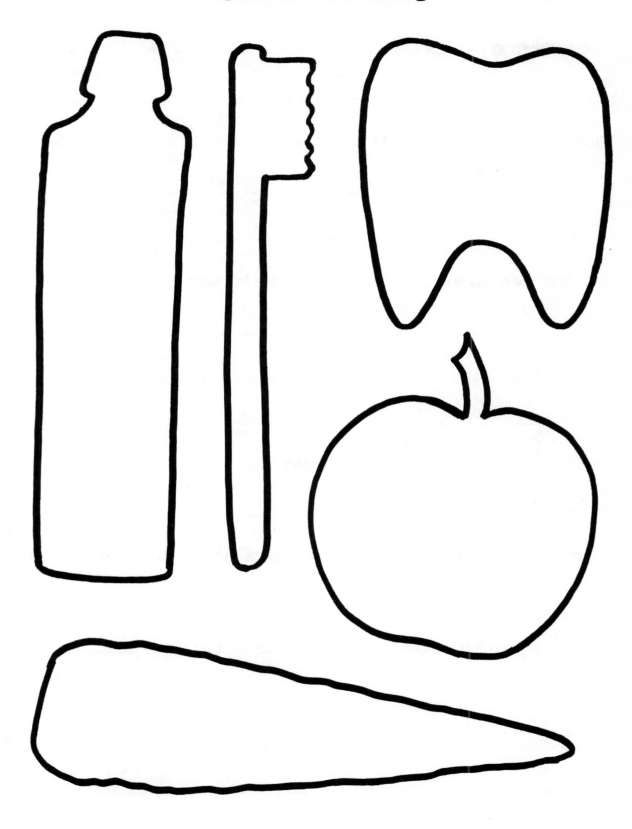

Story Frame: *Doctor DeSoto*

The problem in this story is _____

_____

Doctor DeSoto was going to help the fox because _____

_____

_____

The first thing Doctor DeSoto did to help the fox was _____

_____

Then he had to _____

_____

He knew the fox wanted to eat him because _____

_____

Even though he was afraid, Doctor DeSoto let the fox come back because

_____

After giving the fox a new tooth, Doctor DeSoto told him _____

_____

Doctor DeSoto's problem was solved because _____

_____

Name _____

Help the Tooth

Help the teeth walk down their paths. Two teeth are happy.
One tooth is sad. Do you know why?

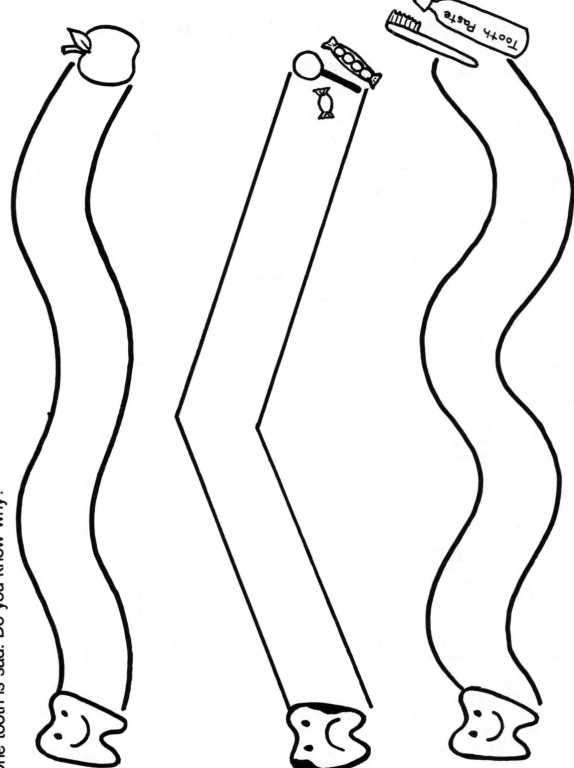

Name _____

Munchy Misfits

One food in each row is not good for your teeth. Put an X on it.

1			
2			
3			
4			
5			

From *Learning Through Literature*, published by Scott, Foresman and Company.
Copyright © 1991 Mary Jane Butner, Jane Ann Peterson, and Janice Marks Sieplinga.

Toothbrush Dot-to-Dot

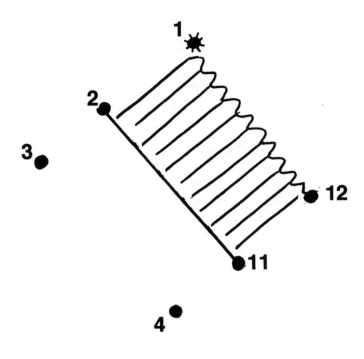

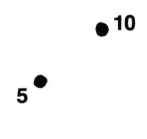

The Path to Healthy Teeth

Follow the path to the healthy tooth.
Stay away from sweet treats!

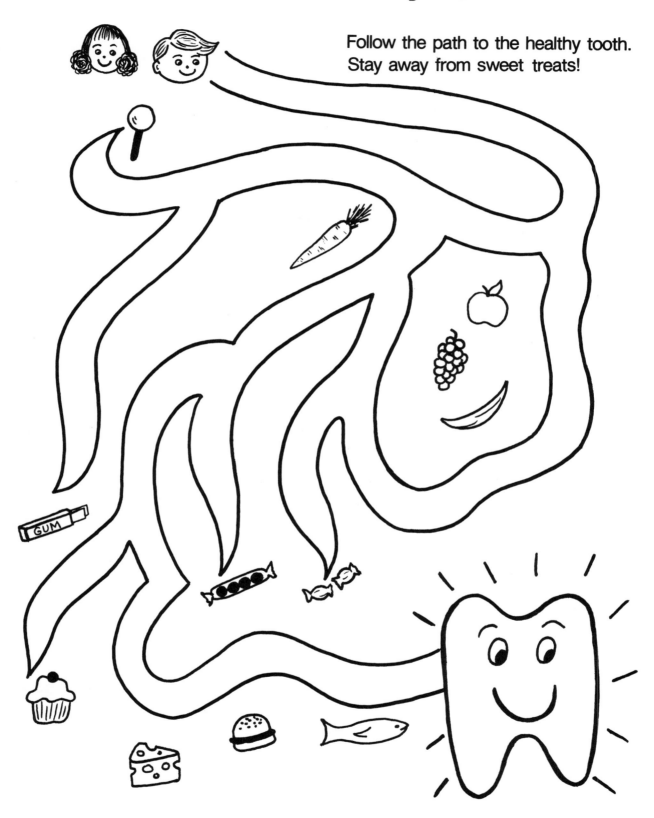

A Tooth Tale

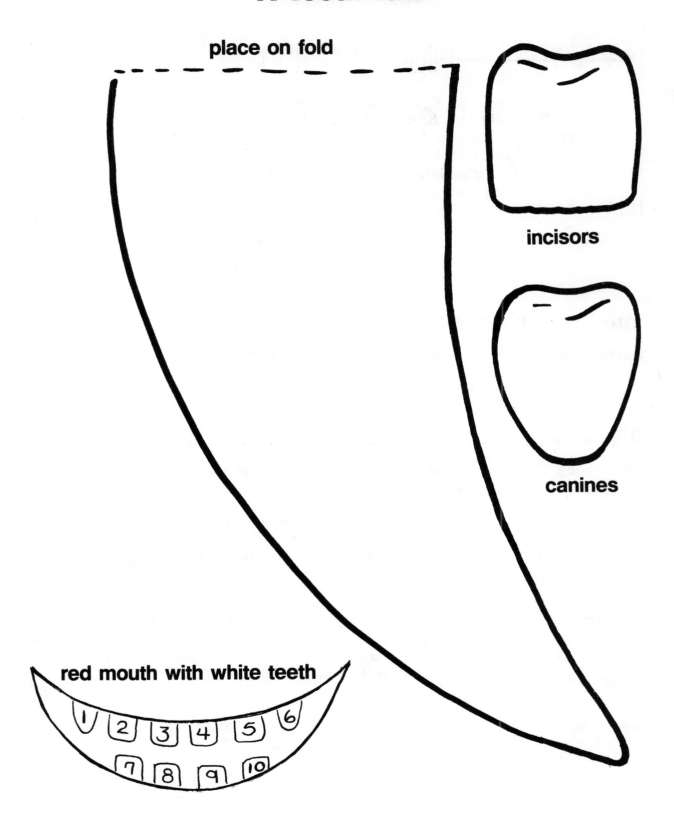

place on fold

incisors

canines

red mouth with white teeth

1 2 3 4 5 6
7 8 9 10

FIREFIGHTER

The Great Big Fire Engine Book, Golden Press, Western
Publishing Company, 1950.
    The alarm bell rings and the firefighters are on their way. This
    book, featuring large colorful pictures and a simple text, shows
    how firefighters use their equipment to put out the fire.

Introductory Activity

Surprise Box   Put a small toy fire truck in the surprise box.

Art Activities

*Fire Truck   Provide each child with a 3¾x10-inch piece of construction
                          paper the same color as your local fire trucks. Older
                          children can trace around a tagboard pattern you make
                          from the worksheet; younger children may need to cut
                          from a pattern pre-traced onto the paper. Have the
                          children cut out two wheels from black paper and put
                          them on the truck with paste or paper fasteners.
                              The children may want to add details—hoses, ladders,
                          firefighters, etc.—to finish the truck. In drawing the ladder,
                          younger children may need you to provide the two
                          horizontal lines to which they can add the rungs. To allow
                          more room for drawing details, you can enlarge the fire
                          truck to 6x18 inches.

---

*Indicates activity that has an accompanying reproducible worksheet.

Firefighter's Hat

This activity is especially fun because the children can wear their fire hats home. Start by giving each child a 12x18-inch piece of red construction paper. Then guide them through the following procedure:

 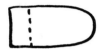

1. Cut one end in a curve (half circle).

2. Fold the opposite end down about 5 inches.

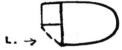 

3. Fold the left corner into the center so that it forms a right triangle.

4. Repeat step 3 with the right corner.

5. Cut out and staple the badge from the "Firefighting Bear" pattern to the hat. Be sure to include the number of your town's fire station on the badge.

*Firefighting Bear

Have the children cut out the bear and his outfit, paste on his hat and jeans, draw a face, and fasten on his badge and shovel. Older children may want to print "SMOKEY" on the bear's hat. Explain that Smokey is the bear who fights forest fires.

*Smokey the Bear Puppet

Reproduce the hat pattern on yellow construction paper and the bear's head on brown. After the children cut out the puppet parts, have them add facial features and paste the hat to Smokey's head. Older children may want to print "SMOKEY" on the hat. When the parts are finished, the children can glue them to a tongue depressor to make a stick puppet.

*Indicates activity that has an accompanying reproducible worksheet.

From *Learning Through Literature*, published by Scott, Foresman and Company. Copyright © 1991 Mary Jane Butner, Jane Ann Peterson, and Janice Marks Sieplinga.

Language Development

Words to Grow By

alarm	axes
pole	net
chief	crank
hoses	chop
hook and ladder	

Something to Think About

How do firefighters know when there is a fire?

What things do firefighters use to fight the fire?

How do they use these things?

What does the fire chief do at the fire?

If people were trapped in a burning building, how do you think the firefighters would get them out?

List in order the things firefighters do to fight a fire.

How do you think the fire might have started?

Do you think that being a firefighter is a dangerous job? Tell why or why not.

How do you think the firefighters feel after the fire is out? Tell something from the story that proves your answer.

Dramatic Play

Provide fire hats, rain slickers, boots, and hoses for dramatic play. The children will provide the siren noises!

Role-Playing Situations

Present these situations to the children and have them tell—or show—what they would do.

1. Pretend that there is a fire at school. Practice the fire drill plan.
2. Pretend that your house is on fire. What should you do? (Tell your parents, leave the house, call the fire station from a neighbor's house, etc.)
3. Pretend that the smoke alarm goes off in the middle of the night. If you smell smoke and it is hard to see, what should you do? (Bend down low or crawl to get under the smoke and leave the house.) If you touch the door and it is hot, what should you do? (Do not open the door. Go to a window. Remember to use your family's fire escape plan.)

*Indicates activity that has an accompanying reproducible worksheet.

4. Pretend that you are sitting around a campfire roasting marshmallows. If your clothes accidentally catch on fire, what should you do? (Stop, drop, and roll.)
5. Pretend that you are Smokey the Bear. What things do you say? ("Only YOU can prevent forest fires." "Do not play with matches or lighters." "Make sure that your campfire is completely out.")

Talk About Burns

Ask the children whether they have ever been burned, how it happened, and what things at home could cause a burn. Then discuss treatment for burns. Tell the children that for minor burns (skin reddened but not broken, no blisters, and covering just a small area) they should run cold water over the area for several minutes, cleanse with plain white soap and water, apply a wet baking soda paste or a mild burn ointment, and cover with a sterile bandage. In case of a major burn, wrap the burned area in a blanket or sheet and get to a hospital at once.

Fine and Gross Motor Skills _____

*Firefighter Seriation and Matching

Use the patterns of fire hats, coats, and trucks to combine fire safety awareness and readiness skills.

For a seriation activity, make the firefighting items in three different sizes, laminate, and have the children take turns putting them in order from the smallest to the largest.

For a visual discrimination activity, use the largest size hat, coat, and truck pattern, making four of each. Have two plain fire trucks and two with ladders; make two plain hats and two with numbers; make two plain coats and two with pockets. Have the children put them in pairs.

*Help the Firefighter and Smokey

Give a copy of the worksheet to each student. By helping the firefighter and Smokey find the items they need, the children will gain practice in left to right readiness.

Indicates activity that has an accompanying reproducible worksheet.

*Firefighters   Have the children circle the items associated with firefighting.

Stop, Drop, and Roll   Children need to be taught that if their clothes catch on fire, they should not run; they should STOP, DROP, and ROLL. Make large signs to reinforce this important safety rule.

Bend Low Under the Smoke   This game helps teach young children to bend low under the smoke when leaving a room that is on fire. Have two people hold a sheet to simulate smoke. As they practice bending low to walk underneath the sheet, have the children sing the following song to the tune of "Swing Low, Sweet Chariot":

Bend low under the smoke,
Bend down very low.
Bend low, down to the ground,
Bend down very low.

Ladder Walk   Bring a ladder to class and lay it flat on the floor. Let the children walk on the rungs, between the rungs, on the sides, etc. If a real ladder is unavailable, you can make one out of masking tape.

Fingerplays and Songs

Ten Little Firefighters
by Mary Jane Butner

Ten little firefighters, all sleepy heads;
But when they hear the fire bell, they jump out of bed.
They get their hats and boots and coats and slide down the pole.
Hurry, hurry, hurry so the fire trucks can roll!

---

*Indicates activity that has an accompanying reproducible worksheet.

Firefighters
by Mary Jane Butner
(Tune: "London Bridge")

The firefighter gets her boots,
Gets her boots, gets her boots.
The firefighter gets her boots.
She has to put the fire out!

(After singing the first verse, let the children make up other verses that tell what the firefighter wears and what she will use to fight the fire.)

(Last verse—sing slowly.)
Now she has put the fire out,
Fire out, fire out.
Now she has put the fire out.
Back she goes to the fire house.

Fire Safety
by Jane Peterson
(Tune: "Bus Song")

The firefighter helps our community.
He will protect you and me.
He wants to keep us safe from harm.
He'll come in a hurry when you sound the alarm.

The firefighter wants us to recall,
When clothes catch on fire
"STOP, DROP, and ROLL!"
If a room is smoke filled—
"BEND LOW or CRAWL!"
And "NEVER PLAY WITH FIRE!"

---

*Indicates activity that has an accompanying reproducible worksheet.

Cooking _____

Firefighter's Hose Cinnamon Rolls

Give each child a section from a package of refrigerated biscuit dough. Have them roll the dough to make long firefighter's "hoses." Then tell them to coil the dough in a circle and dip it in melted margarine and cinnamon sugar. Place the hose rolls on a baking sheet and bake 8-10 minutes at 425°.

"Telesquirt" Punch

Substitute diet Squirt for the water needed to mix with a can of frozen punch concentrate. "Telesquirt" is a make of snorkel fire truck.

Science _____

Fire Experiments

Have the children sit at a safe distance around a table as you demonstrate the following experiments involving fire.
1. Light a candle stub and let it burn out. Ask the children why the flame went out. (Answer: There was no fuel left to burn.)
2. Light another candle and let a child blow it out. Again ask the children why the flame went out. (Answer: The child's breath pushed the heat away, lowering the temperature of the candle.)
3. Relight the candle and put a glass over it. Ask once more why the flame went out. (Answer: There was no more oxygen to keep it burning.)

Math _____

*Counting Firefighting Gear

Make felt cutouts using the patterns from "Firefighter Seriation and Matching." Have the children use them to do flannelboard counting and math.

---

*Indicates activity that has an accompanying reproducible worksheet.

From *Learning Through Literature*, published by Scott, Foresman and Company.
Copyright © 1991 Mary Jane Butner, Jane Ann Peterson, and Janice Marks Sieplinga.

Kindling Temperatures	Older children can research the kindling temperatures of common materials and graph their findings. Here are some examples of materials and their kindling temperatures: paper, 450°F. (232°C.); cellophane, 468°F. (242°C.); wood, 375-510°F. (190-266°C.); cotton, 511°F. (266°C.); wood alcohol, 867°F. (464°C.); natural gas, 900-1170°F. (482-632°C.)

Extended Experiences

Field Trip	Take the children on a trip to the fire station.
Resource Person	Invite a firefighter to visit the class. Some fire departments will send a fire truck to school for a presentation. Check with your local fire station.
Firefighter Show and Tell Day	Have the children bring toy fire hats, fire trucks, books, and puzzles about fire safety.

Related Books

The Big Book of Real Fire Trucks and Fire Fighting, Teddy Slater, Grosset and Dunlap, 1987.
> Realistic pictures and descriptive text cover firefighters and their history, trucks, and equipment.

Curious George at the Fire Station, Margaret Rey and Alan J. Shalleck (eds.), Houghton Mifflin Company, 1985.
> Curious George finds out about firefighters and, as usual, gets into mischief!

Fire Engines, Anne Rockwell, E. P. Dutton, 1986.

Fire! Fire! Gail Gibbons, Harper and Row, 1984.
> This book explains how different kinds of fires are fought in the city, country, forest, and on the waterfront.

Hercules, Hardie Gramatky, G. P. Putnam, 1940.
> Although Hercules is an old-fashioned horse-drawn firetruck, he still can be useful when the modern trucks fail!

Indicates activity that has an accompanying reproducible worksheet.

190

Fire Truck

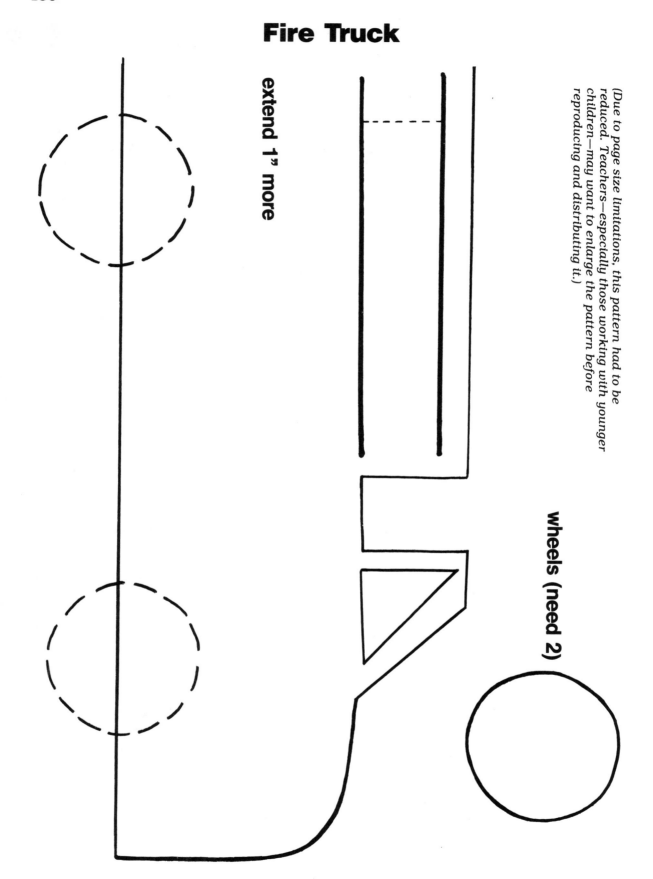

extend 1" more

wheels (need 2)

Firefighting Bear

Firefighting Bear

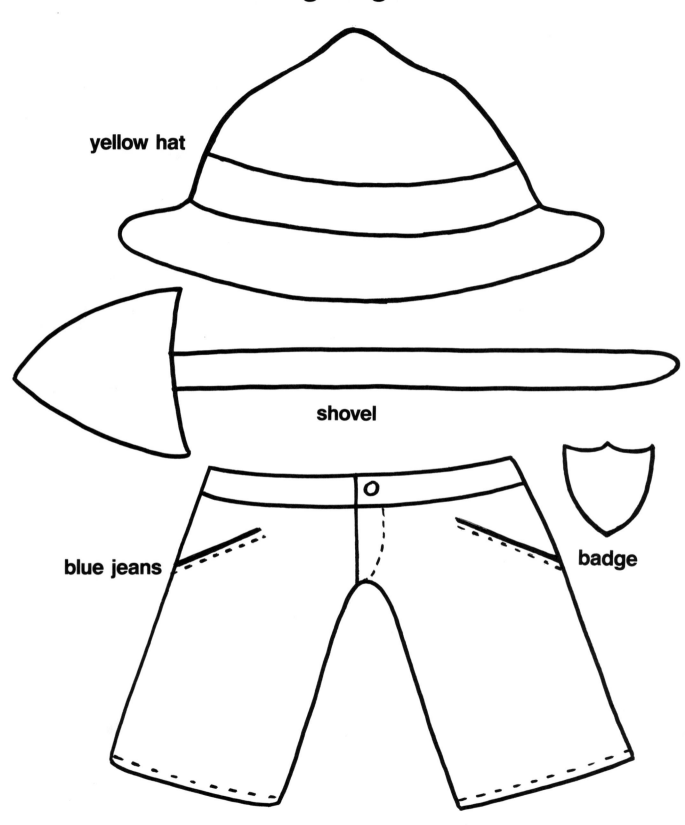

yellow hat

shovel

blue jeans

badge

Smokey the Bear Puppet

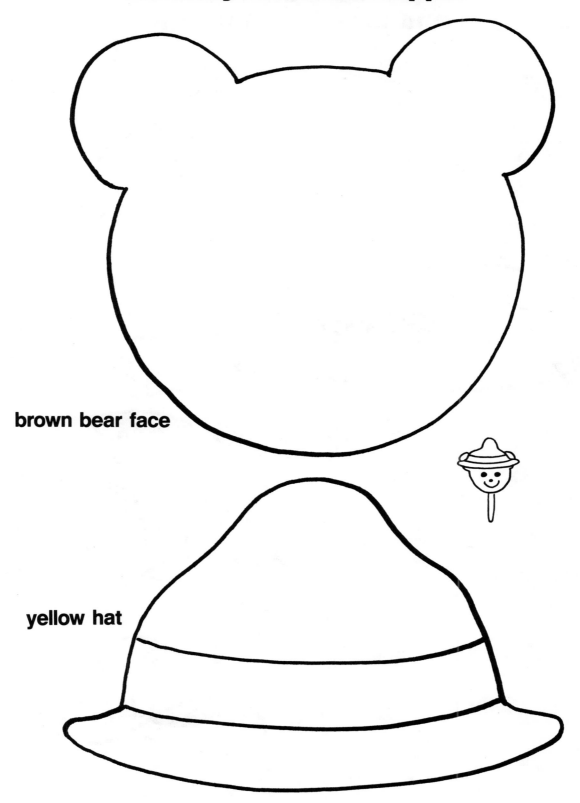

brown bear face

yellow hat

Firefighting Seriation and Matching Patterns

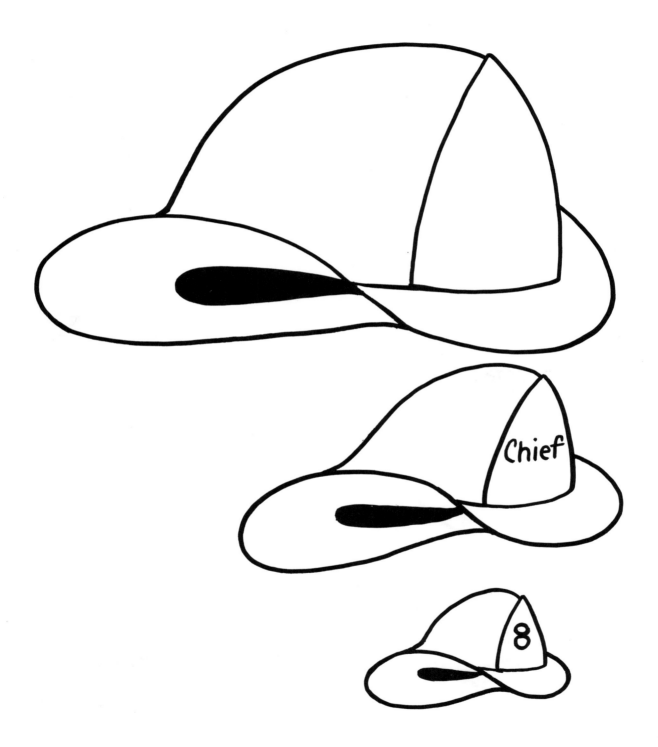

Firefighting Seriation
and Matching Patterns

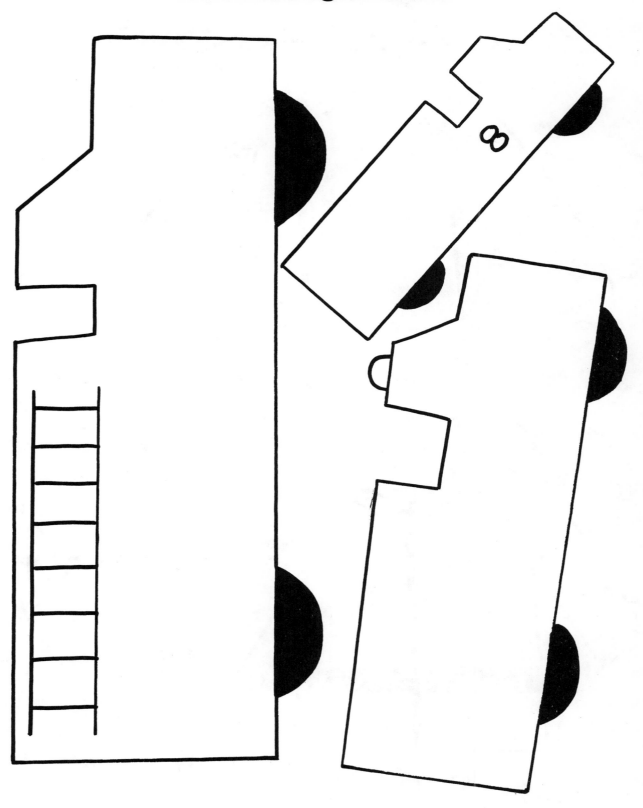

Firefighting Seriation and Matching Patterns

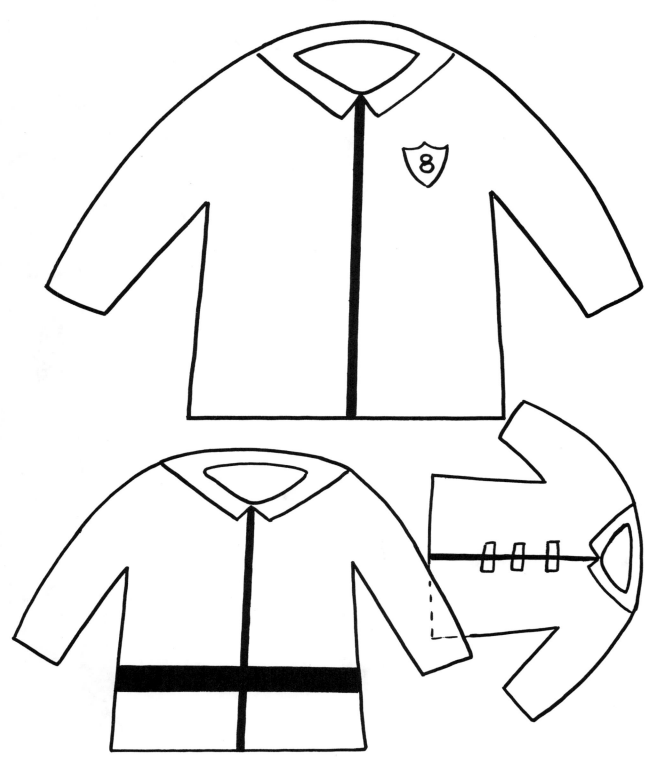

Name

Help the Firefighter and Smokey

Help the firefighter go to the fire.

Help Smokey find his shovel.

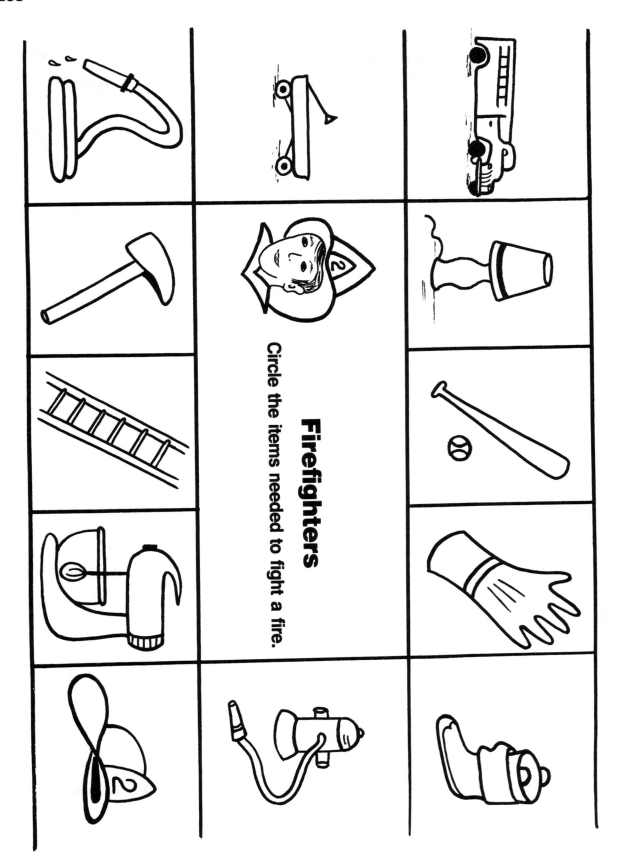

198

Name _____

Firefighters

Circle the items needed to fight a fire.

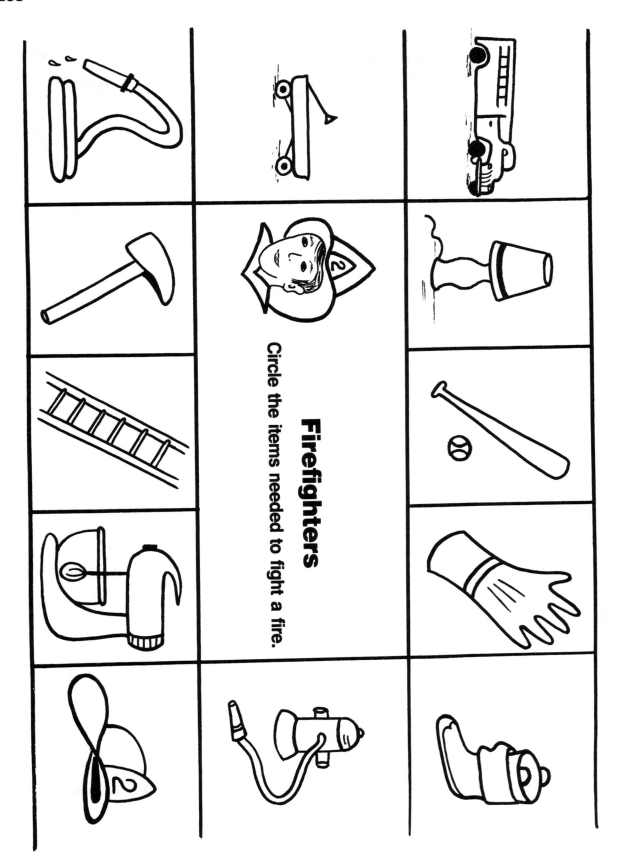

FOLK TALES

Handprint Hen
The Little Red Hen

Vegetable Prints
Stone Soup

Paper Bag Fish
Six Foolish Fishermen

The Little Red Hen
Six Foolish Fishermen, Benjamin Elkin
Stone Soup, Ann McGovern

The Little Red Hen, Golden Press, Western Publishing Company, 1980.

The Little Red Hen must tend her wheat and bake her bread without the help of her friends. But they come running when it's time to eat the bread! This story, which reinforces the concept of cooperation, lends itself to easy dramatization due to its repetitive form.

Introductory Activities

Surprise Box

Put some seeds, a small loaf of bread, or a sheaf of wheat in the surprise box.

*Clothespin Puppets

The directions for clothespin puppets are given in detail on the pattern pages. You may want to make and laminate a complete set of the puppets for classroom use. Open and shut the clothespins to have each animal introduce itself to the children.

Glove Puppet

You can make miniature versions of the story characters out of felt and pompons. Attach one character to each finger of a glove, and either you or the children can wear the glove to help tell the story.

*Indicates activity that has an accompanying reproducible worksheet.

From *Learning Through Literature,* published by Scott, Foresman and Company.
Copyright © 1991 Mary Jane Butner, Jane Ann Peterson, and Janice Marks Sieplinga.

Art Activities

*Clothespin Puppets

The directions for making these puppets are given in detail on the pattern pages. The children may choose to do one character or several.

*Little Red Hen Stick Puppet

Have the children cut out the hen, apron, and hat, paste the parts together, and glue the puppet to a tongue depressor.

Seed Collage

Save and dry a variety of seeds for the children to use in making collages.

Handprint Little Red Hen

Dip the child's hand in red tempera or fingerpaint and then onto paper to make a handprint. Be sure to extend the child's thumb away from the fingers. When the paint dries, the child can add a beak, feet, and eye.

Thumbprint Chick

Press a child's thumb onto a stamp pad—or into yellow tempera—and then onto paper to make a thumbprint. The child can then use a fine-tip marker to draw the chick's features.

*Indicates activity that has an accompanying reproducible worksheet.

Language Development _____

Words to Grow By   grain   dough
                       reap   knead
                       sickle   rise
                       scythe   yeast
                       mill   cooperation
                       grinds   lazy
                       miller   ambitious

**Something to
Think About**

What did the Little Red Hen find?

What did she do with the seed?

Who were the Little Red Hen's friends?

Why didn't she share the bread with them?

How would the story have been different if her friends had
    helped the Little Red Hen?

Which job do you think was the hardest? the easiest?

For which job do you think the Little Red Hen needed the
    most help?

What would you say to your friends if they didn't help you
    with some hard work?

Do you think the Little Red could have persuaded her
    friends to help her? If so, how?

Storytelling

The repetitive form of *The Little Red Hen* makes it an
easy story for children to retell. To help them remember
the characters and the details of the story, show them
some flannelboard figures, clothespin puppets, or a glove
puppet. With very young children, you may want to retell
the story and have the children respond "Not I!" at the
appropriate times.

*Tools

Use the patterns to make flannelboard cutouts. Then ask
the children which tool the Little Red Hen needed first,
second, and so on.

_____

*Indicates activity that has an accompanying reproducible worksheet.

***Little Red Hen Sequence**	Have the children cut out the pictures and paste them on the loaf of bread to help them recall the sequence of events in *The Little Red Hen*.
***Little Red Hen Story Map**	Do this story map as a group activity with younger children and as an independent activity with older children.

Fine and Gross Motor Skills _____

Play Dough	Let the children pretend that the play dough you give them is real dough that they can form into rolls and loaves of bread. Also provide toy rolling pins, bread pans, and muffin pans.
Barnyard Scramble	Give each child a sticker showing a farm animal, but limit the variety of animals to just two or three. At a signal, have all the children walk around the classroom making the sounds of their animals and listening for others making the same sounds. As they find each other, they hold hands and stay together as a group. The game is over when all the children are in the correct animal groups.
Here Chick, Chick, Chick	Choose one child to be the farmer and several other children to be the chicks. The chicks stand in a row in front of the farmer who feeds each one some cereal in the sequence you say—e. g., "the first chick . . . the third chick . . . the fifth chick . . . the second chick . . . ."
Feed the Chicks	Scatter pegs or bingo markers on the floor. The children are chicks and try to pick up all the pieces of "chicken feed" in a given time period.

_____

Indicates activity that has an accompanying reproducible worksheet.

Fingerplays and Songs _____

Little Red Hen
by Mary Jane Butner

Hickety, pickety, Little Red Hen,
She bakes bread now and then;
Sometimes nine loaves, sometimes ten,
Hickety, pickety, Little Red Hen.

Hickety, pickety, duck and pig,
Like to sing and dance a jig.
They won't plant and they won't dig.
Hickety, pickety, duck and pig.

Hickety, pickety, goose and cat,
Said, "We won't help—and that is that!"
While Hen was working, they just sat!
Hickety, pickety, goose and cat.

Making Bread
by Jane Peterson
(Tune: "Mulberry Bush")

This is the way we plant the seed,
Plant the seed, plant the seed.
This is the way we plant the seed
So early in the morning.

This is the way we cut the wheat,
Cut the wheat, cut the wheat.
This is the way we cut the wheat
And take it to the mill.

The mill grinds the wheat into flour;
Into flour, into flour.
The mill grinds the wheat into flour;
Now we can go home.

Now it's time to mix the bread,
Knead the bread, let it rise.
Now it's time to bake the bread.
Look, it's getting brown!

_____

Indicates activity that has an accompanying reproducible worksheet.

The best part is to eat the bread,
Eat the bread, eat the bread.
The best part is to eat the bread;
But now I'm getting full!

Traditional   *Old McDonald's Farm*
                       The Farmer in the Dell

Cooking

Bread   Let the children help mix and knead the ingredients, using
                       a packaged bread mix. If cooking facilities are not available
                       at school, ask a parent who bakes bread to provide a loaf—
                       preferably uncut so the children can see what it looks like
                       before you slice it.

Butter   Put a small amount of whipping cream in a baby food jar
                       so that it is about 1/4 full. You can have a jar for each
                       child or have two or three children share a jar and take
                       turns shaking it. As the children shake, cream will first
                       coat the sides of the jar and then clear by itself. In five to
                       ten minutes (depending on how hard the Little Red Hen
                       and her friends work!), a lump of butter will be visible in
                       the buttermilk. Drain off the buttermilk and put all the
                       lumps of butter in a bowl. Beat the butter with a spoon,
                       rinse it several times in cold water, and add salt. Serve
                       with the homemade bread.

Science

Raising Crops   Examine a variety of seeds with a magnifying glass. Plant
                       some wheat seeds (or anything else that grows quickly) at
                       school. Have the children water and tend the plants and
                       measure the growth.

*Indicates activity that has an accompanying reproducible worksheet.

Liquids and Solids   If you make butter in class, have the children observe and then describe how the cream changes from a liquid to a solid. They may also observe and comment on the change in color that occurs.

Math ⎯⎯⎯⎯⎯⎯⎯⎯⎯⎯⎯⎯⎯⎯⎯⎯⎯⎯⎯⎯⎯⎯⎯⎯⎯⎯

*Largest to Smallest   In this seriation activity, have the children put the hens and chicks in order from the largest to the smallest.

Graph—1   If you plant seeds, have the children record the growth on a graph.

Graph—2   If you had the children make clothespin puppets, ask them "Which animal did you choose to make?" Record their answers on a graph.

*Little Red Hen's Garden

Make a copy of the worksheet for each child. You can then use the worksheet in several different ways. Here are some suggestions.

1. Work on a specific number, such as 4. Give each child some kernels of corn. Ask the children to put four kernels in each row. When the children have mastered one number concept, repeat the activity with another number.

2. Give the children manipulative experiences with addition and subtraction by telling this story:

   The Little Red Hen was walking down the road and found three seeds. She picked them up. (Have the children pick up three kernels of corn.) She walked a little farther and picked up four more seeds. (Children pick up four more kernels.) How many seeds does she have now?
   The Little Red Hen planted five of the seeds in her garden. (Have the children lay five kernels on the worksheet.) How many does she have left?

---

*Indicates activity that has an accompanying reproducible worksheet.

She found two more seeds over by the fence. (Children pick up two more.) How many does she have now? She plants four. (Children lay four on the worksheet). How many are left? How many seeds has the Little Red Hen planted in her garden altogether?

3. Have the children work on different combinations of a specific number, such as 10. Give each child 10 kernels of corn and ask them how many different ways they can "plant" the seeds in two rows (two in one row, eight in the other; three and seven; etc.). Encourage older children to write appropriate equations ($2 + 8 = 10$, $3 + 7 = 10$, etc.).

Extended Experiences _____

Field Trips   Take the children on a trip to a farm, a bakery, or a supermarket.

Related Books _____

Good Morning, Chick, Mirra Ginsburg, Scholastic Book Services, 1980.
   An egg cracks open and out comes a chick. He sets off to explore the barnyard.

That's What Friends Are For, Florence Parry Heide and Sylvia Worth Van Clief, Scholastic Book Services, 1968.
   Theodore the elephant has hurt his foot and can't walk. Everyone gives him advice until one friend suggests that what he really needs is *help.*

Who Took the Farmer's Hat?, Joan L. Nodset, Scholastic Book Services, 1963.
   The farmer has lost his old brown hat. And bird just found a beautiful new brown nest!

Indicates activity that has an accompanying reproducible worksheet.

From *Learning Through Literature*, published by Scott, Foresman and Company.
Copyright © 1991 Mary Jane Butner, Jane Ann Peterson, and Janice Marks Sieplinga.

Clothespin Puppets

Directions: Cut out the head. Fold *in* on the center lines and *out* on the other lines to make a wedge-shaped mouth. Paste the beak (hen, duck, or goose) inside the wedge—the beak will protrude. Attach the body. Glue a clip clothespin to the back of the wedge to make the mouth open and shut.

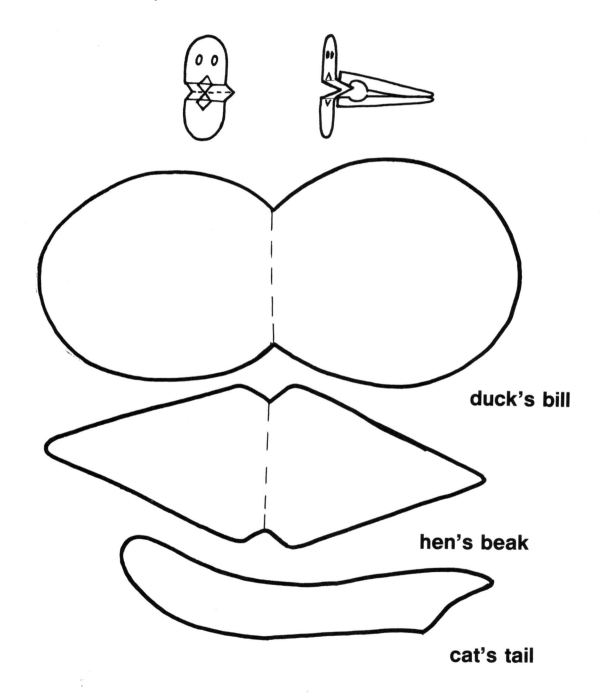

duck's bill

hen's beak

cat's tail

Clothespin Puppets
Little Red Hen

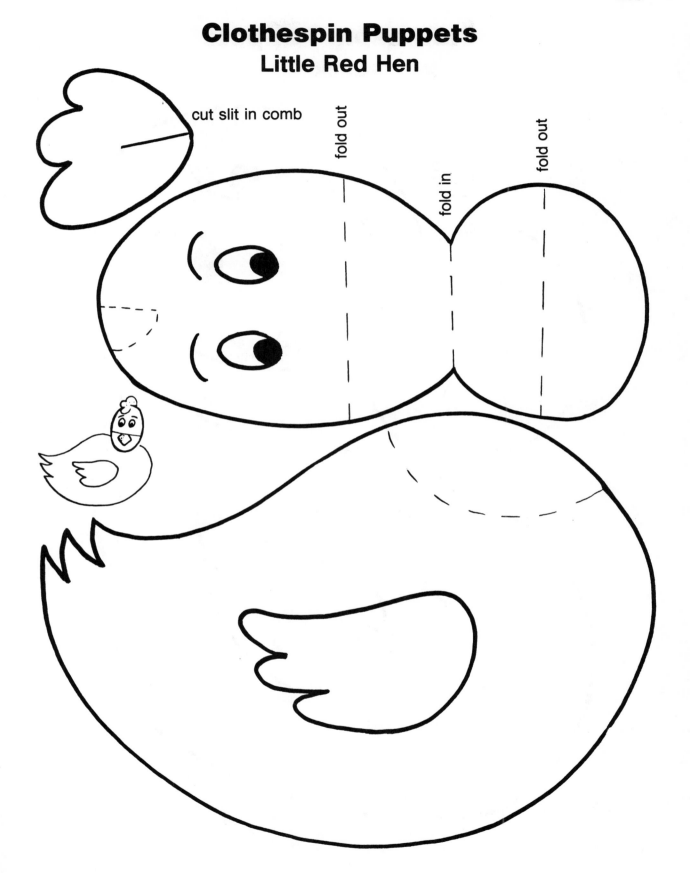

cut slit in comb

fold out

fold in

fold out

Clothespin Puppets
Duck

Clothespin Puppets
Pig

pig's tail—
cut in spiral

Clothespin Puppets
Cat

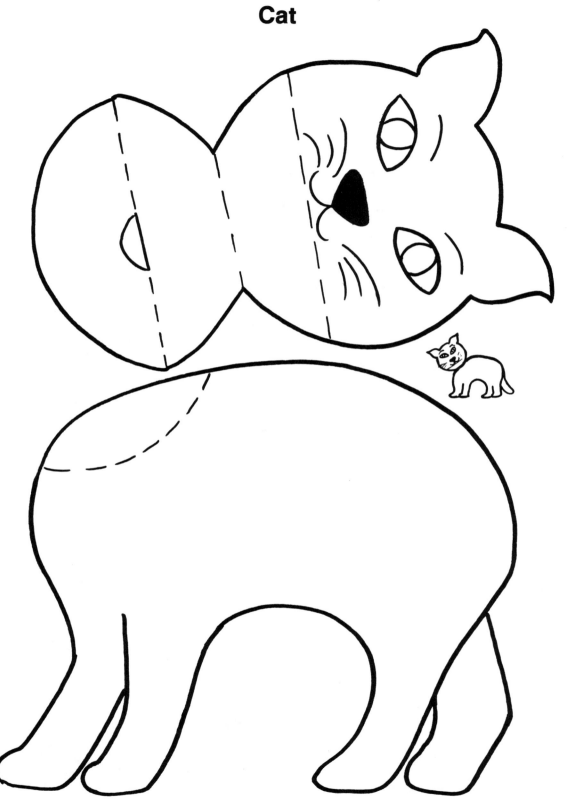

Clothespin Puppets
Goose

body

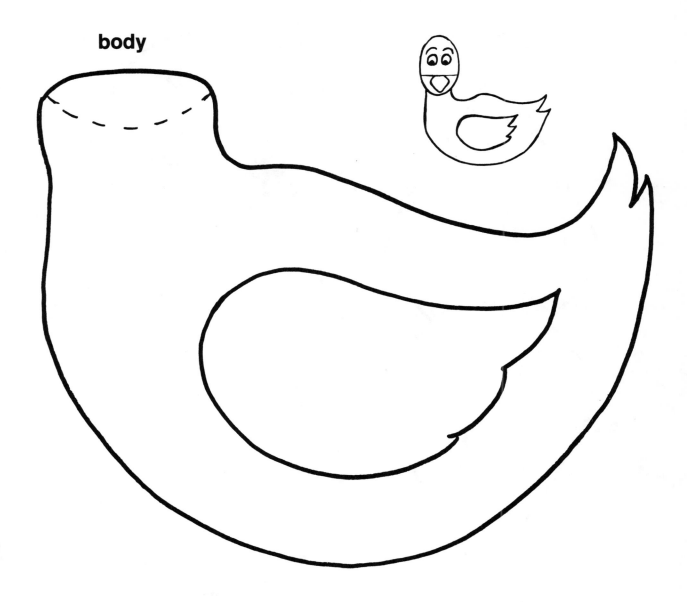

Clothespin Puppets
Goose

head

beak

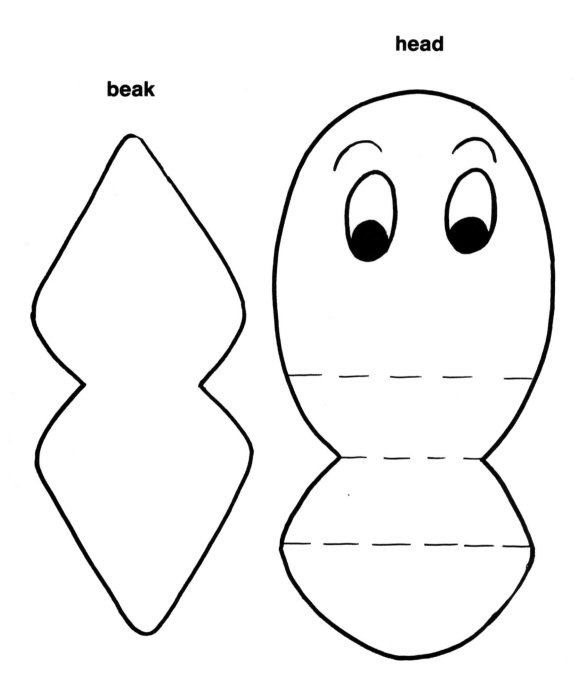

Little Red Hen Stick Puppet

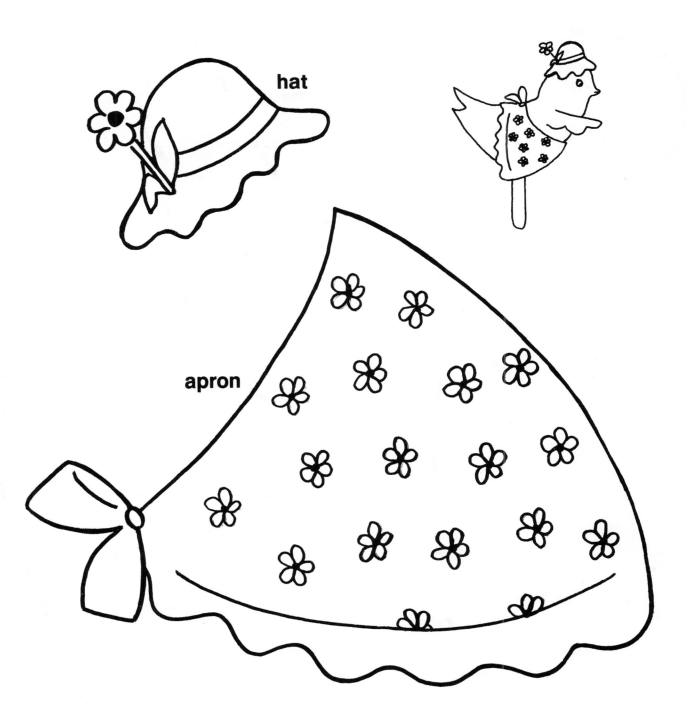

hat

apron

Little Red Hen Stick Puppet

Tools

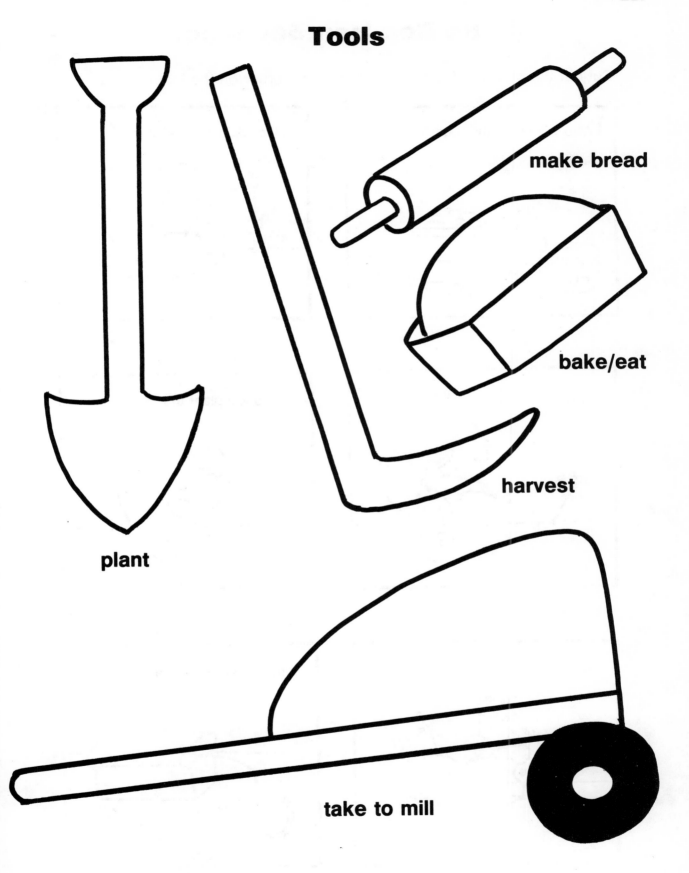

make bread

bake/eat

harvest

plant

take to mill

Little Red Hen Sequence

Cut out the pictures. Paste them in the right order on the loaf of bread.

Who will make the bread?

Who will cut the wheat?

Who will go to the mill?

Who will plant the seed?

Who will bring the flour home?

Who will eat the bread?

Name _____

Little Red Hen Sequence

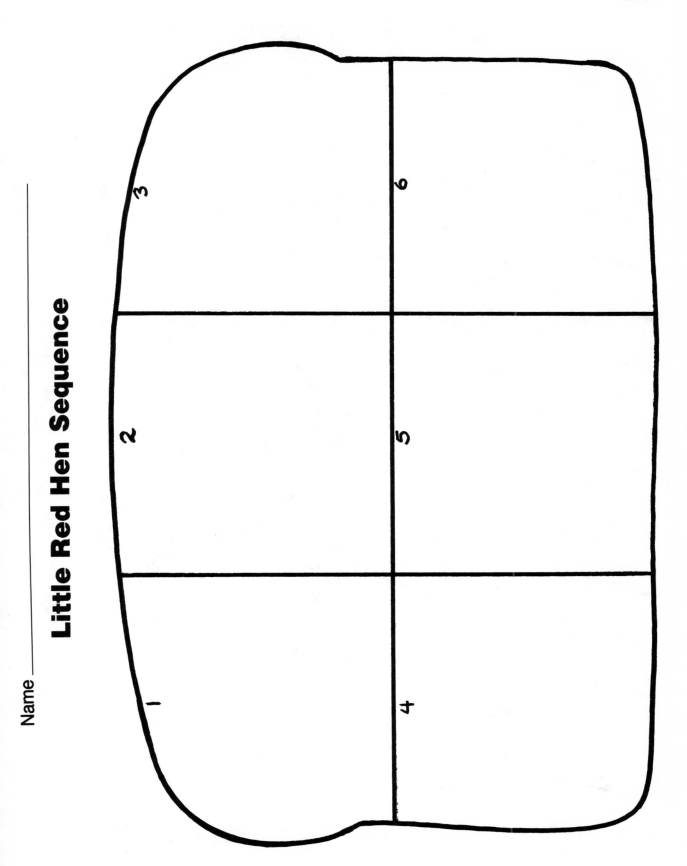

220

Name _____

Little Red Hen Story Map

Let's remember what happened in the story.

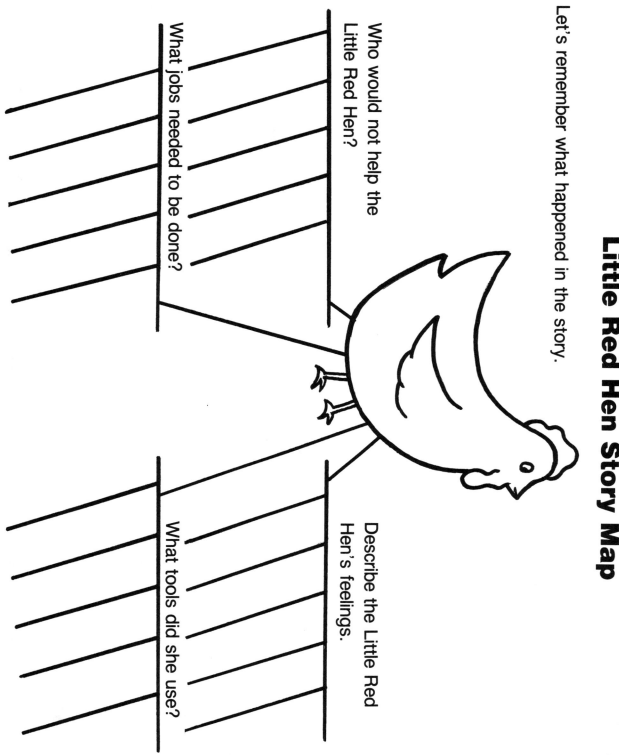

Who would not help the Little Red Hen?

What jobs needed to be done?

Describe the Little Red Hen's feelings.

What tools did she use?

Largest to Smallest

add legs

Largest to Smallest

add legs

Little Red Hen's Garden

Six Foolish Fishermen, Benjamin Elkin, Childrens Press, 1957.

Poor fishermen! All the brothers think that one has drowned because each counts to five and forgets to count himself.

Introductory Activity

Surprise Box

Put a fishing reel or bobber inside the surprise box. When all the children have had a chance to feel the object and guess what it is, ask the children where they would usually see this item.

Art Activities

Crayon Resist

Have the children use crayons to draw fish. Tell them to press down hard on their crayons. Then have them paint over their pictures with watered-down blue paint.

Textured Fish

Let the children glue elbow macaroni to paper cut in a fish shape.

Underwater Scene

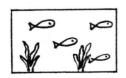

Add a few drops of blue food coloring to a mixture that is half water and half glue. Brush the glue mixture all over a sheet of white drawing paper. Now lay thin strips of green tissue paper "seaweed" on the glue, brush more of the glue mixture on top, and let dry. Cut sponges into fish shapes, dip them in paint, and press on the background.

---

*Indicates activity that has an accompanying reproducible worksheet.

Fish Bowl

Provide each child with two paper plates, clear plastic wrap, and some goldfish crackers. Have the children cut out the center of one plate and tape the clear plastic wrap over the opening. Then have them paint the other plate blue, and—before stapling the plates together—place the goldfish crackers inside. The children can shake their "bowl" and see the fish "swimming."

Fish Mobile

Make fish from 2x12-inch strips of paper. Cut slits on opposite sides of the strip one inch from each end so that they interlock when folded around. Dangle several fish from strings. Vary the size of the strips to make bigger or smaller fish.

Paper Bag Fish

Lightly stuff the bottom of a small paper bag. Tie off the bottom with string to form the fish's tail; then stuff the rest of the bag, forming the fish's body, before tying off this section with more string. Paint.

Language Development

Words to Grow By

foolish
accepted
drowned
eldest
gratefully
include

woe
merry
sorrow
shrieked
raft

Something to Think About

Where was each brother fishing?
Why did each think a brother was missing?
Is anyone missing from your class? Count carefully!

*Fish Facts

Do this story map as a group activity with younger children. With older children, make a copy for each child to work on independently.

---

*Indicates activity that has an accompanying reproducible worksheet.

Dramatization   This story is an excellent vehicle for potential dramatic actors. Children can have fun pretending to cry when they think a brother is missing. Don't be surprised if the children have trouble keeping straight faces while crying!

Reading Readiness   Label some large cutouts that show where the brothers were fishing—e. g., "in a boat," "on a log"—and then use the cutouts as scenery when dramatizing the story.

Fine and Gross Motor Skills _____

*Trace the Fish   Make a copy of the worksheet for each child. Tracing the fish provides practice in fine motor skills.

*A MAZEing Fish   As they follow the maze, children develop tracking, small muscle control, and decision-making skills.

*Find the Fish   Make a copy of this visual discrimination activity for each child in the class.

Fishing   Make many fish of different colors and sizes, laminate, and attach paper clips at their mouths. Tie one end of a string to a magnet. Tie the other end to a dowel. Scatter the fish on the floor, and let the children use the "fishing pole" to catch them.

Water Play   Put some toy boats in a tub of water, and let the children gently blow the boats around. You can also let the children make their own toy boats out of pieces of Styrofoam and attach sails with toothpicks.

_____

*Indicates activity that has an accompanying reproducible worksheet.

Row the Boat   Put the children in pairs and have them sit facing each
                          other with their feet together and holding hands. At a
                          signal, the children start gently rocking back and forth
                          while singing "Row, Row, Row Your Boat." When they
                          finish, they release their partners "jump overboard and
                          swim around," and link up with new partners. Then they
                          repeat the activity.

Fingerplays and Songs

Six Little Fish
by Mary Jane Butner

Six little fish swimming in the brook
One got caught on a fisherman's hook.
Hurry up fisherman—put him in the pan.
Fry him up and eat him as fast as you can!

(Repeat with five, four, three, two, and one fish.)

Fisherman
by Mary Jane Butner
(Tune: "Oh Where Has My Little Dog Gone?")

Oh where, oh where has the fisherman gone?
Oh where, oh where can he be?
Is he in the boat or on the bridge?
Or did he fall into the sea? KERSPLASH!

Oh where, oh where has the fisherman gone?
Oh where, oh where can he be?
Is he on a log or on the bank?
Or did he fall into the sea? KERSPLASH!

Oh where, oh where has the fisherman gone?
Oh where, oh where can he be?
Is he on a stump or on the rock?
Or did he fall into the sea? KERSPLASH!

Indicates activity that has an accompanying reproducible worksheet.

Cooking

Tuna Salad   The children can chop onions and celery, mix them with tuna and mayonnaise, and spread their tuna salad on bread or crackers for a snack.

Fish Pretzels   Mix the following ingredients together in a large bowl:
   1 package yeast
   1½ cups warm water
   1 Tbsp. sugar
   1 tsp. salt
Stir in 4 cups of flour and knead until smooth. Give the children pieces of dough to roll into ropes and twist into fish shapes. Brush the dough with beaten egg and sprinkle with salt. Bake at 425° for 15 minutes or until the pretzels are brown.

Science

Aquarium   Maintaining a classroom aquarium is a good ongoing activity. Goldfish are easy to care for and fun to watch. Tropical fish are more varied, but they require a heated tank. Let the children take turns feeding the fish.

Sink or Swim   Show the children various objects and ask them to predict which ones will float and which ones will sink. After they make their predictions, let them place the objects—one at a time—in a tub of water. Challenge the children to find ways to keep the sinking objects afloat.

Indicates activity that has an accompanying reproducible worksheet.

Math _____

**Big Fish,
Little Fish**

Using the fish of various sizes from the "Fishing" activity, have the children compare fish by length. They can also use rulers to measure the fish and then lay the fish in order from smallest to largest. In addition, you can mark each fish with dots to denote weight—the more dots the heavier the fish. Have each child catch a fish, count the dots, and then stand in a line that goes from the heaviest fish to the lightest fish.

Estimating

Older children can estimate the length of the fish from "Big Fish, Little Fish" and then check their estimates by measuring.

Beanbag Fish

Make some fish-shaped beanbags of different sizes and weights for the children to measure and weigh.

Attendance

Let the children take turns counting the class members each day. Don't be surprised if, like the fishermen, some forget to count themselves.

*Shape Fish

Use the patterns to make a large collection of posterboard fish in various geometric shapes: circle, triangle, square, and rectangle. Laminate the fish. Make "ponds" in the same four shapes, and have the children sort the fish by shape and place them in the appropriate ponds.

Extended Experiences _____

Field Trips

Take the children on a field trip to an aquarium, a fish hatchery, or a pet shop that sells fish. You might also take them to a market where freshly caught fish are sold or to a trout pond where they could actually go fishing.

---

*Indicates activity that has an accompanying reproducible worksheet.

From *Learning Through Literature*, published by Scott, Foresman and Company.
Copyright © 1991 Mary Jane Butner, Jane Ann Peterson, and Janice Marks Sieplinga.

Related Books

Swimmy, Leo Lionni, Pantheon (Random House), 1968.
> The beauties of marine life as seen through the eyes of a little lost fish.

The Magic Fish, retold by Freya Littledale, Scholastic Book Services, 1967.
> A story of greed, ambition, overweening pride, and tragic downfall.

Indicates activity that has an accompanying reproducible worksheet.

Name _____

Story Map: Fish Facts

Where can you fish?

rivers

What can you use as bait?

Name some fish.

Trace the Fish

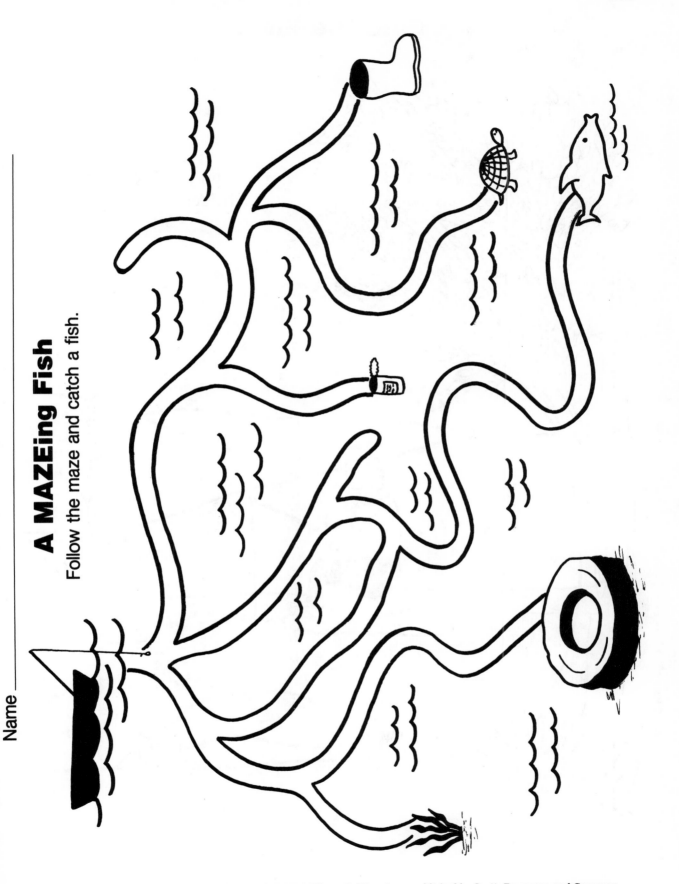

Name —————————

A MAZEing Fish
Follow the maze and catch a fish.

Find the Fish

Can you find the six fish hidden in the picture?

Shape Fish

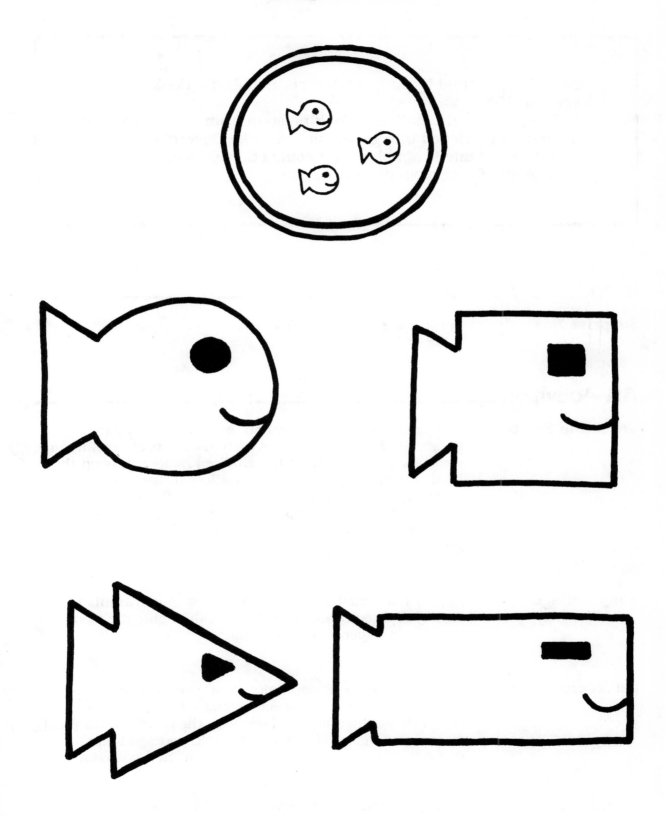

Stone Soup, retold by Ann McGovern, Scholastic Book Services, 1968.

Intrigued by the notion of making soup from a stone, an old woman is tricked into generosity. Ann McGovern's retelling of this old tale is simpler than some other versions—easy listening for very young children.

Introductory Activity

Surprise Box   Put a stone in the surprise box.

Art Activities

*Vegetable Prints   Give each child a kettle cut out of black construction paper. Slice some vegetables—onions, peppers, mushrooms, radishes, etc.—and have the children make prints on the kettle by dipping their vegetable slices in paint and then pressing them onto the paper. Cut vegetables such as carrots, celery, and peppers both lengthwise and across, and ask the children to compare the different prints made from the same vegetable.

*Soup Collage   Supply rice, dried peas, different kinds of macaroni, and a variety of dried beans. Have the children glue the food items on a paper cutout of a stone.

Pet Rocks   Before taking the children out for a walk, tell them that they are each to find a special stone—their pet rocks. When they return to the classroom, the children can paint on faces and glue on movable eyes. Encourage them to name their pets and to display them in the classroom.

*Indicates activity that has an accompanying reproducible worksheet.

Rock Animals   Have the children glue together rocks of various sizes to form sculptures of real or imaginary animals. Let them paint, decorate, and name their creations.

Rock Designs   Give each child several small stones to drop on a piece of paper to form a "connect the dots" pattern. Have the child use a crayon to draw in the lines between the stones. Encourage the children to repeat the activity several times, using a different color crayon each time, to create an interesting design.

Language Development

Words to Grow By   selfish   barley
                        generous   ingredients
                        stir

Something to Think About
                         What ingredients went into the soup?
                         Why did the old woman say she had no food?
                         Why did she finally help the young man?
                         At the end of the story, the young man says, "What a fine supper I will have tomorrow." What do you think he will have for supper tomorrow?
                         Do you think the stone was an important ingredient in the soup? Why or why not?

Recipes   Have older children write down their versions of how to prepare their favorite foods. Younger children can dictate their recipes to an adult.

*Dramatization   Select one child to be the young man and another to be the old woman. Have other children hold large cutouts of the ingredients from the "Stone Soup" song activity and jump into the pot (a circle on the floor) as the old woman adds them to the soup. Remind the children to use the old woman's phrase: "Soup from a stone, fancy that!"

*Indicates activity that has an accompanying reproducible worksheet.

From *Learning Through Literature*, published by Scott, Foresman and Company.
Copyright © 1991 Mary Jane Butner, Jane Ann Peterson, and Janice Marks Sieplinga.

***Structured Story
Starter**

Encourage the children to write their own versions of *Stone Soup*. Ask them what "trick" they will use to start the soup and what other ingredients they will put in. Who will make the soup? Where will the story take place?

*Stone Word Game

This activity provides older children with practice in spelling, phonics, and printing as they try to make as many words as possible from the letters in "stone."

Fine and Gross Motor Skills _____

*Dot-to-Dot Pot

Give each child a copy of the worksheet. Have the children connect the dots and then draw the soup ingredients in the pot.

**Pouring and
Coordination**

Provide pots, bowls, soup ladles, measuring cups, and spoons. Fill a dishpan with water, another with rice, and another with beans. Let the children practice filling containers and then emptying them back into the appropriate dishpan. Have the children note that some materials weigh more than others even though they are in the same size measuring cups. They should also note that the various materials sound different as they are poured.

Stepping Stones

Lay some blocks on the floor and have the children step from one to another, keeping their balance as they pretend to cross a brook.

Cross the River

Glue ten "stones" numbered from 1 to 10 on a long piece of blue craft paper. Have the children cross the "river" by stepping on the stones whose numbers you call out: "Step on 3, go to 6, to 9, to 10." You can make this game more challenging by giving the children a series of numbers to remember before they start.

Indicates activity that has an accompanying reproducible worksheet.

Rock Relay Divide the class into teams. Give one child from each team a rock and a spoon. The child then carries the rock on the spoon, deposits the rock in a bucket, runs back, and passes the spoon to the next person on the team. That person must repeat the activity with a different rock.

Fingerplays and Songs

Soup Chant
by Mary Jane Butner

Stir the soup and stir the soup and stir it in the pot.
Stir the soup and pour it out and eat it while it's hot.

Stone Soup
by Mary Jane Butner and Jane Peterson
(Tune: "Alouette")

Stone soup, we are making stone soup.
Get a little stone and put it in the pot.
Put the stone in the pot, put the stone in the pot.
In the pot, in the pot. Ohhhhh!

Stone soup, we are making stone soup.
Get a lot of water and put it in the pot.
Put the water in the pot, put the water in the pot.
With the stone, with the stone,
In the pot, in the pot. Ohhhhh!

Stone soup, we are making stone soup.
Get some yellow onions and put them in the pot.
Put the onions in the pot, put the onions in the pot.
With the water, with the water,
And the stone, and the stone,
In the pot, in the pot. Ohhhhh!

Stone soup, we are making stone soup.
Get some skinny carrots and put them in the pot.
Put the carrots in the pot, put the carrots in the pot.

*Indicates activity that has an accompanying reproducible worksheet.

With the onions, with the onions,
And the water, and the water,
And the stone, and the stone,
In the pot, in the pot. Ohhhhh!

Stone soup, we are making stone soup.
Get a fat chicken and put it in the pot.
Put a chicken in the pot, put a chicken in the pot.
With the carrots, with the carrots,
And the onions, and the onions,
And the water, and the water,
And the stone, and the stone,
In the pot, in the pot. Ohhhhh!

Stone soup, we are making stone soup.
Get a juicy beef bone and put it in the pot.
Put a beef bone in the pot, put a beef bone in the pot.
With a chicken, with a chicken,
And the carrots, and the carrots,
And the onions, and the onions,
And the water, and the water,
And the stone, and the stone,
In the pot, in the pot. Ohhhhh!

Stone soup, we are making stone soup.
Get some salt and pepper and put them in the pot.
Put salt and pepper in the pot, salt and pepper in the pot.
With a beef bone, with a beef bone,
And a chicken, and a chicken,
And the carrots, and the carrots,
And the onions, and the onions,
And the water, and the water,
And the stone, and the stone,
In the pot, in the pot. Ohhhhh!

Stone soup, we are making stone soup.
Get some yellow butter and put it in the pot.
Put some butter in the pot, put some butter in the pot.
With the salt and pepper, salt and pepper,
And a beef bone, and a beef bone,
And a chicken, and a chicken
And the carrots, and the carrots,
And the onions, and the onions,
And the water, and the water,
And the stone, and the stone,
In the pot, in the pot. Ohhhhh!

Stone soup, we are making stone soup.
Get a little barley and put it in the pot
Put the barley in the pot, put the barley in the pot,
With the butter, with the butter,
Salt and pepper, salt and pepper,
And a beef bone, and a beef bone,
And a chicken, and a chicken,
And the carrots, and the carrots,
And the onions, and the onions,
And the water, and the water,
And the stone, and the stone,
In the pot, in the pot. Ohhhhh!

Stone soup, we have made some stone soup.
Get a bowl and spoon—come and eat it while it's hot!

Cooking

Stone Soup

Make stone soup with the class. Assign each child one item to add to the soup: carrots, celery, onions, potatoes, 2-4 cans of beef broth, salt and pepper, 1/2 cup of rice, and—of course—one gourmet cooking stone. Start with 3 cups of water in an electric cooker. To save time, you may want to heat the water before class. Make sure the children are watching as you drop the stone into the water. Then in go the cans of broth followed by the cut-up vegetables, rice, salt, and pepper. Have the children take turns stirring and remarking, "Soup from a stone—fancy that!" Cooking time is approximately 30 minutes, when everything but the stone should be tender!

Science

Rocks

Display various rocks (available from museum gift shops and rock exhibitions). Try to have some that are polished, some in their natural state, and some that contain fossils. Encourage older children to try to match polished and unpolished specimens of the same rock. Let younger children simply enjoy looking at and feeling the rocks or examining the fossils.

Indicates activity that has an accompanying reproducible worksheet.

Math

Counting

Collect some empty soup cans and write a number on the outside of each one. Have the children drop a corresponding number of small stones into each can. With younger children who don't yet recognize numbers, put a matching number of dots next to each number. They can then drop in as many stones as there are dots on the can.

Rock Sorting

Collect three empty coffee cans with plastic lids. Make holes of different sizes in the lids. Then have the children drop stones of the appropriate size through the lids—small stones through the small hole, etc. When they finish dropping all the stones, they can count and compare the amounts in each container.

Extended Experiences

Field Trip

Visit a restaurant that specializes in making soup.

Resource People

Invite a chef to visit the class and discuss soup-making. Or have a parent who makes homemade noodles help the class prepare chicken noodle soup from scratch. You might also ask a rock collector to come in and tell the children about interesting rock specimens that can be found locally.

Related Books

Chicken Soup with Rice, Maurice Sendak, Scholastic, 1962.
   The months and seasons fly by in rhyme as the narrator enjoys chicken soup with rice.

Indicates activity that has an accompanying reproducible worksheet.

Mexicali Soup, Kathryn Hitte, Parents' Magazine Press, 1970.
   The opposite of *Stone Soup*, this story concerns a family that is
   served plain hot water after all the ingredients are taken out of
   the soup.

Stone Soup, Marcia Brown, Scribner's, 1947.
   In this version, three soldiers teach a whole village how to make
   soup from a stone.

Stone Soup, Tony Ross, Dial Books, 1987.
   In this sly and hilarious version, a little hen whets a wolf's
   curiosity about stone soup and not only avoids being eaten by
   him but also gets him to do her household chores!

Indicates activity that has an accompanying reproducible worksheet.

Vegetable Prints

kettle

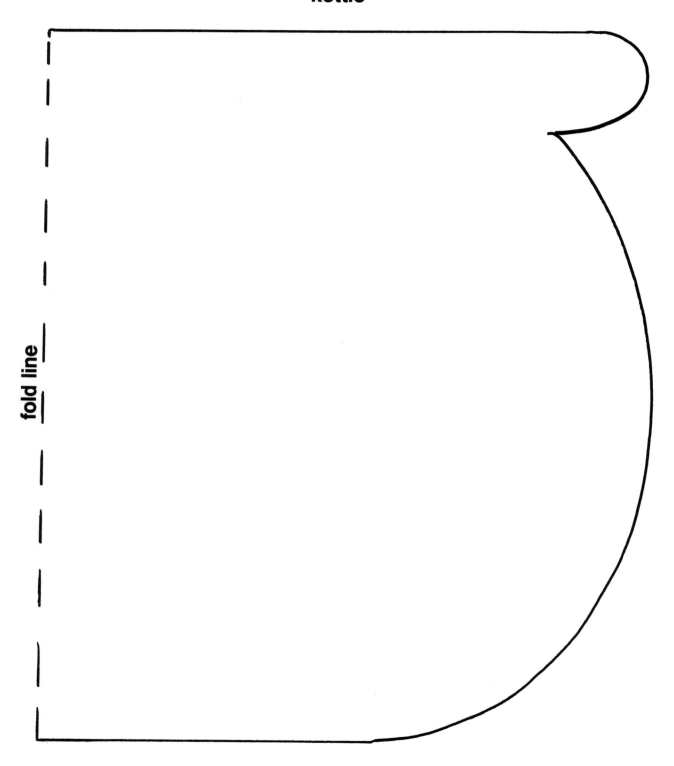

fold line

Soup Collage

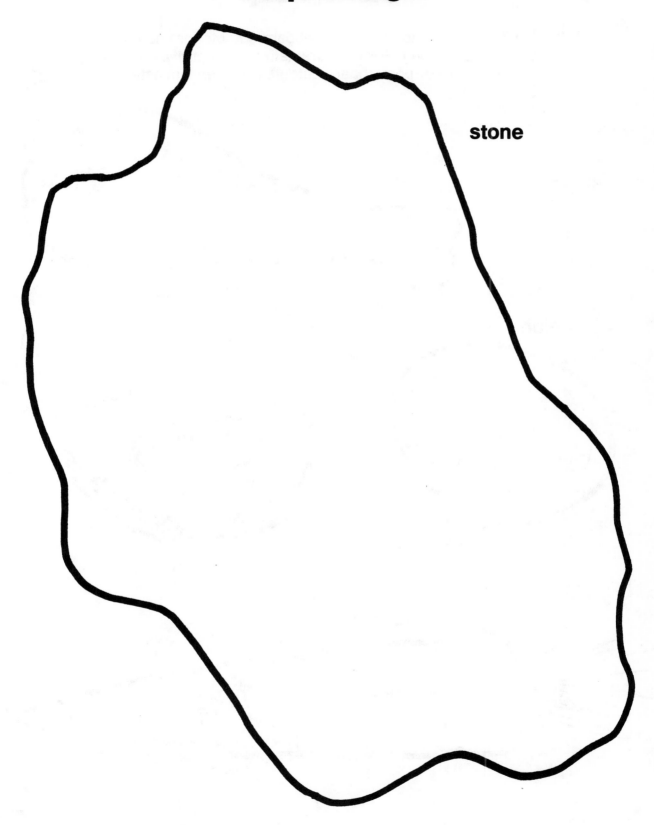

stone

Stone Soup

Use the patterns to make flannelboard cutouts for use in the "Stone Soup" song. For the "Dramatization" activity, use the patterns to make posterboard cutouts and then laminate.

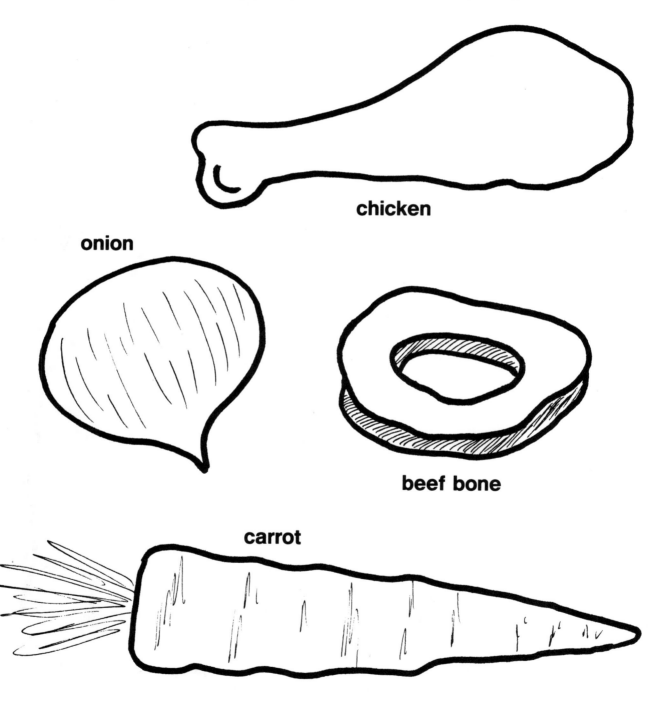

chicken

onion

beef bone

carrot

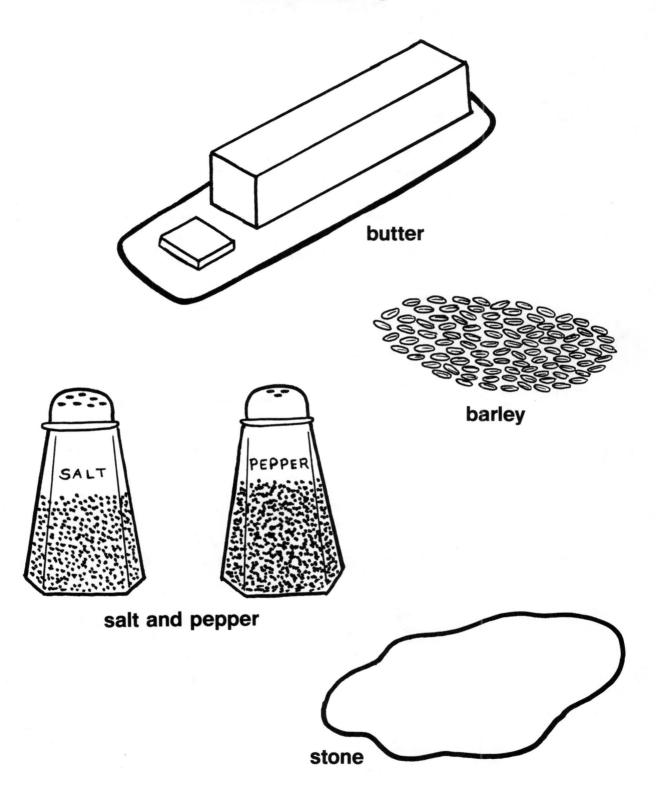

Stone Soup

butter

barley

salt and pepper

stone

Structured Story Starter:
Stone Soup

My soup will start with a _____

The characters in my soup story are _____

_____

_____

The characters are making the soup because _____

_____

_____

These things will go into my soup: _____

_____

_____

This is how it all happened:

_____

_____

_____

_____

_____

Name _____

Stone Word Game

How many words can you make out of the word "stone"?

STONE

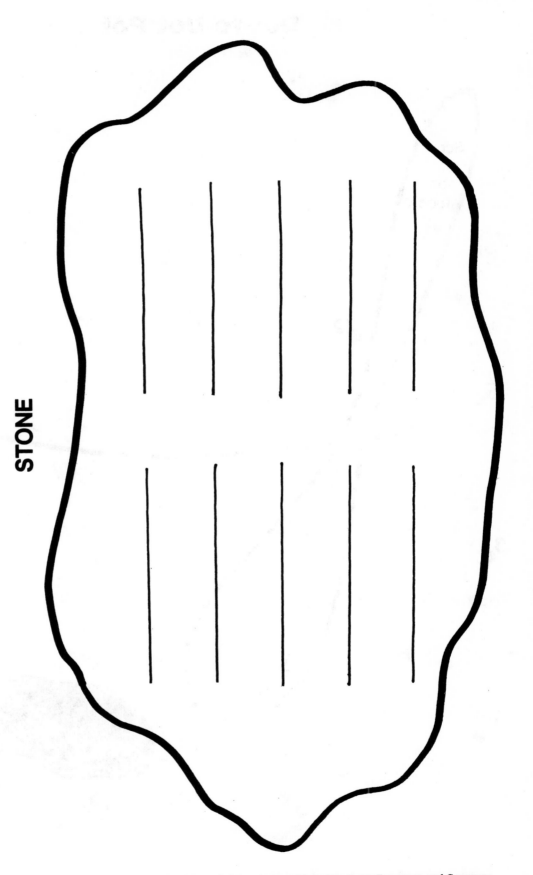

Dot-to-Dot Pot

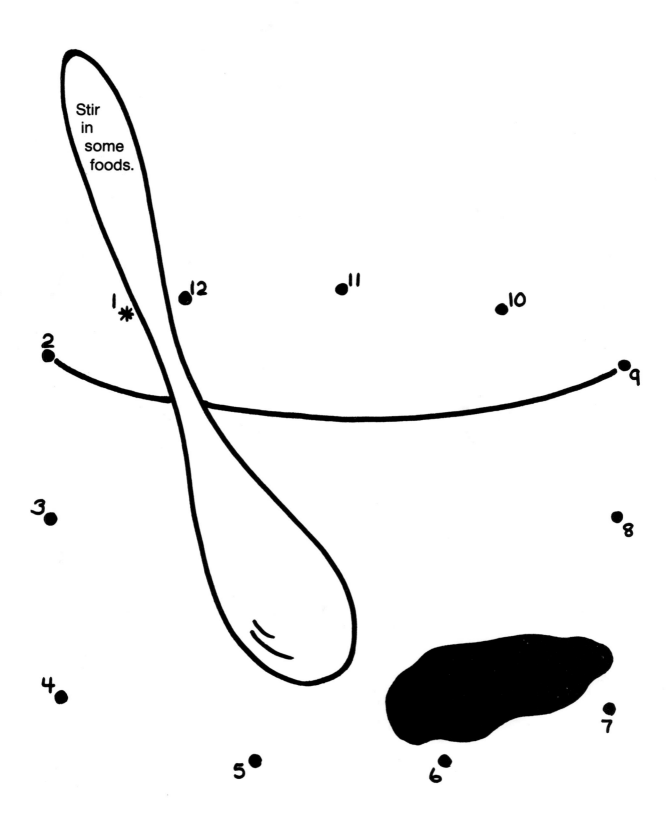

Stir in some foods.

SEASONS

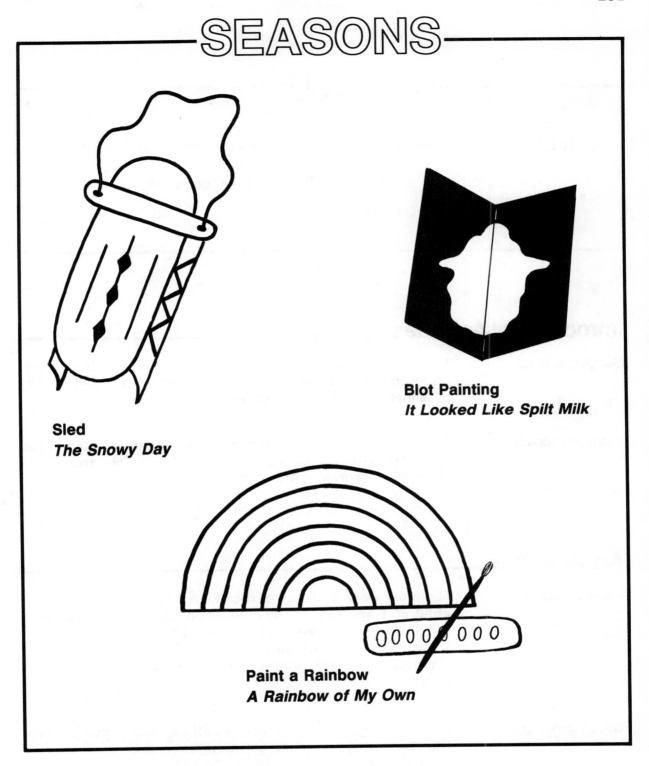

Sled
The Snowy Day

Blot Painting
It Looked Like Spilt Milk

Paint a Rainbow
A Rainbow of My Own

It Looked Like Spilt Milk, Charles G. Shaw
The Snowy Day, Ezra Jack Keats
A Rainbow of My Own, Don Freeman

From *Learning Through Literature*, published by Scott, Foresman and Company.
Copyright © 1991 Mary Jane Butner, Jane Ann Peterson, and Janice Marks Sieplinga.

```
┌─────────────────────────────────────────────────────────────┐
│                       ═══ FALL ═══                          │
│                                                             │
│  It Looked Like Spilt Milk, Charles G. Shaw, Harper and Row, │
│  1947, 1988.                                                │
│      Look! Up in the sky! It's a rabbit! It's an ice cream  │
│  cone! It's a . . . cloud!                                   │
│                                                             │
└─────────────────────────────────────────────────────────────┘
```

Introductory Activities

Surprise Box   Put cotton balls or cotton batting in the surprise box. The children can describe how the cotton feels. Can they think of something that looks like cotton?

Flannelboard   Prepare felt cutouts of some of the objects mentioned in the story. What do the objects look like? Tell the children that there is a surprise at the end of the story!

Art Activities

*Cloud Pictures   Make tagboard patterns of the cloud shapes. Let the children trace around the cutouts on white paper, cut out the shapes, and paste them on blue paper. Or you can trace the patterns on blue paper and have the children fill them in with chalk, soap paint, cotton balls, or shaving cream.

Blot Paintings   Fold blue construction paper in half and then open it. Have the children spoon white paint on one side of the fold, close the paper, and rub—spreading the paint around. When they open the paper again, have them describe the clouds they have created.

---

*Indicates activity that has an accompanying reproducible worksheet.

Surprise Designs   This activity requires an electric warming tray and, of course, adult supervision. Heat up the warming tray and then lay a piece of white paper on it. Let each child make a design by rubbing a white crayon or a candle over the heated paper. Then take the paper off the tray and allow it to cool. When the paper is cool, each child can complete the design by using a sponge to cover the entire paper with a wash of watered-down blue food coloring.

Tear Paper Clouds   Let each child create a cloud by tearing around the edges of a piece of white paper.

Language Development

Words to Grow By   spilt
great horned owl

Something to Think About   What were some of the things the cloud looked like?
Do you ever look for pictures in the clouds?
What cloud pictures have you seen?
Did you ever go through the clouds?
Have you ever been above the clouds?
Can you touch a cloud? If so, where?
Could you sit on a cloud?
Can clouds cover things up?
What colors can clouds be?

*Story Map   Use this worksheet with younger children as a story chart activity. Older children can fill in the story map independently.

If I Could Float on a Cloud . . .   Record the ideas of younger children. With older children, give them the topic as a creative writing activity.

*Indicates activity that has an accompanying reproducible worksheet.

From *Learning Through Literature*, published by Scott, Foresman and Company.
Copyright © 1991 Mary Jane Butner, Jane Ann Peterson, and Janice Marks Sieplinga.

What's in the Sky?   Ask the children to name as many things as they can think of that can be seen in the sky. Write down their ideas on chart paper.

Writing   Make a pattern book by having the children create their own cloud pictures and using the "*Spilt Milk*" format to describe them. Because the story's vocabulary is so simple and repetitive, your classroom book will be easy enough for even the youngest child to "read."

Fine and Gross Motor Skills _____

*Things We See in the Sky   Make a copy of this visual discrimination worksheet for each child.

Whose Shadow?   Find pictures of real animals and draw a silhouette of each one. Let the children match the picture to the silhouette and clip the pair together with a clothespin.

Chalk Clouds   Encourage the children to draw large clouds on the chalkboard.

Parachute Activities   Provide a white sheet (or a real parachute if possible) and have the children move it gently up and down in time to some "billowy" music. Then, for a change of pace, do the activity to some "thunderstorm" music. Beethoven's Sixth Symphony, the "Pastoral," would be appropriate.

Over and Under the Clouds   Select two children to hold the ends of a long white crepe streamer. Tell them to raise or lower the streamer as you direct the other children to go under or over the clouds.

*Indicates activity that has an accompanying reproducible worksheet.

Cloud Tag   Read "Clouds" by Christina Rosetti (in Fingerplays and Songs below). Then play a stop-and-go game to music. Encourage the children to move lightly and gracefully while the music plays and to remain motionless when the music stops.

Shadow Tag   Go outside on a sunny day and have the children try to step on each other's shadow.

Fingerplays and Songs

Pictures in the Sky
by Jane Peterson
(Tune: "The Animal Fair" American Song)

When I look up in the sky —, I see white clouds float–ing by —.

Some are fluf–fy, bil–low–y, Swirl–ing pic–tures in the sky—.

O–ver there I see ice cream—, Or is it a li–on mean—?

There is a pret–ty bride dressed in white silk—;

And now it looks like spilt milk. Spilt milk, Spilt milk, Spilt milk.

Indicates activity that has an accompanying reproducible worksheet.

Clouds
by Christina Rosetti

White sheep, white sheep
On a blue hill,
When the wind stops
You all stand still.
When the wind blows,
You walk away slow.
White sheep, white sheep,
Where do you go?

Cloud Pictures
by Janice Marks Sieplinga
(Tune: ''The Muffin Man'')

(TEACHER)
Do you see what I can see?
What I can see? What can I see?
Do you see what I can see,
When I look at the clouds?

(CHILDREN)
I can see an ice cream cone,
An ice cream cone, an ice cream cone.
I can see an ice cream cone,
When I look at the clouds.

(Let the children sing about other cloud pictures they remember from It Looked Like Spilt Milk. *Children can also choose a flannelboard cutout from the ''Cloud Pictures'' activity or make up an original cloud picture to sing about.)*

Cooking ────────────────────────────

Berries in a Cloud   Let the children spread whipped topping around on a paper
   plate. Drop strawberries or blueberries onto the topping
''cloud.''

---

*Indicates activity that has an accompanying reproducible worksheet.

Science

Clouds	Display pictures of different kinds of clouds—nimbus, cirrus, cumulus, and stratus. Label and talk about the clouds. Encourage the children to look at real clouds in the sky for several days on their way to and from school. Challenge them to identify the different types of clouds they see.
Weather Chart Graph	Chart the daily weather for a month.
Our Days Are Numbered	If you kept a classroom weather chart, have the children count the number of cloudy, rainy, and sunny days at the end of the month.
Cloud Simulation	Use a humidifier to simulate clouds. The children can experience sitting in a cloud.

Math

***Clouds and Raindrops**	Use the patterns to cut ten clouds from white felt and 55 raindrops from blue paper. Number the clouds from 1 to 10. In this matching game, the children place the correct number of raindrops on each cloud.

Extended Experiences

Looking for Cloud Pictures	Go outside on a pleasant but cloudy day. Tell all the children to lie back in the grass and look for cloud pictures.

Indicates activity that has an accompanying reproducible worksheet.

Related Books

Look Again, Tana Hoban, MacMillan Publishing Company, 1971.
Things are seldom what they seem! Tana Hoban's book shows
extreme close-ups of objects so that children see things from a
new perspective. Then, following each close-up, the object
appears in its normal way.

The Alphabet Symphony, Bruce McMillan, Greenwillow Books, 1977.
Children who are observant can find all the letters of the
alphabet in the instruments of an orchestra.

Is This A Baby Dinosaur? Millicent E. Selsam, Harper and Row,
1971.
This book features close-up photos of objects in nature, followed
by larger pictures and explanations of the objects.

The Cloud Book, Tomie de Paola, Holiday House, 1975.
Children will find a good deal of factual information about clouds
accompanied by Tomie de Paola's charming illustrations.

Indicates activity that has an accompanying reproducible worksheet.

Cloud Pictures

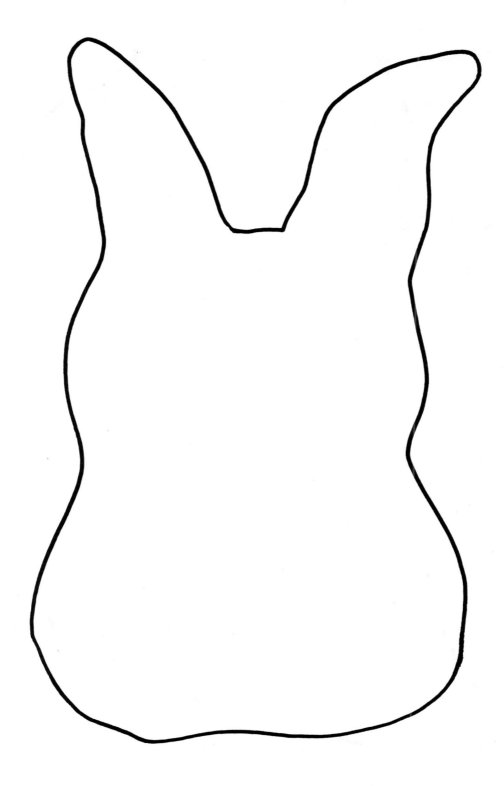

Cloud Pictures

Cloud Pictures

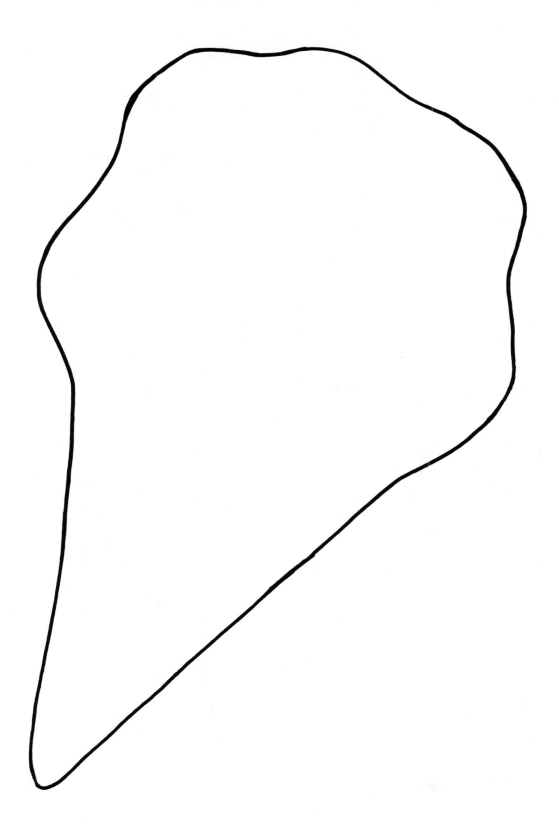

Cloud Pictures

Cloud Pictures

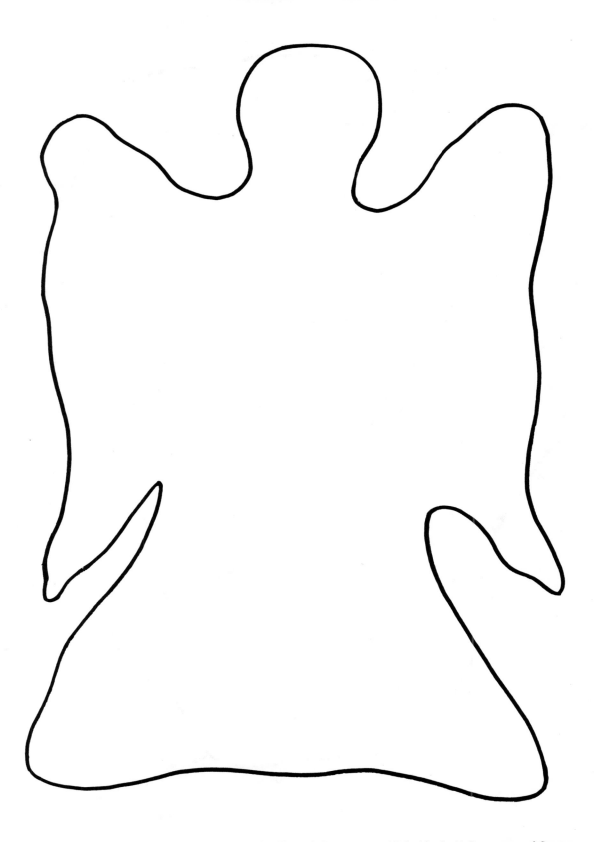

Cloud Pictures

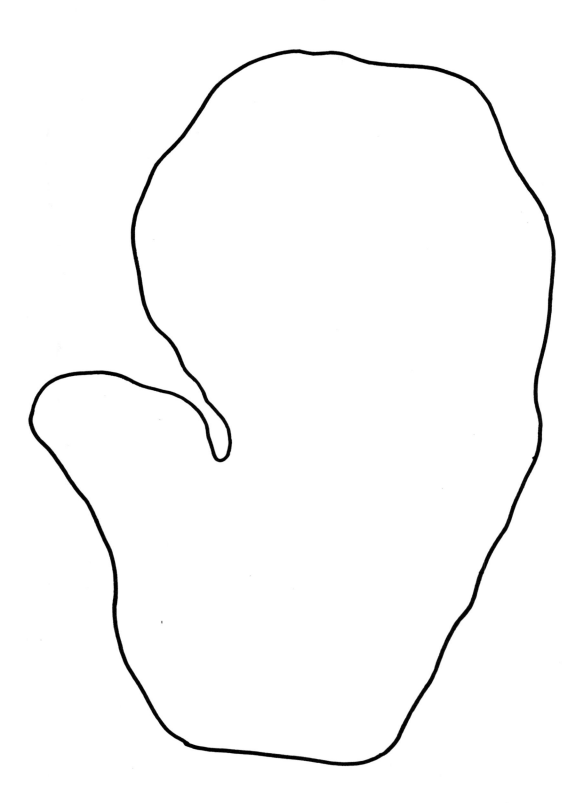

Name _____

Story Map:
It Looked Like Spilt Milk

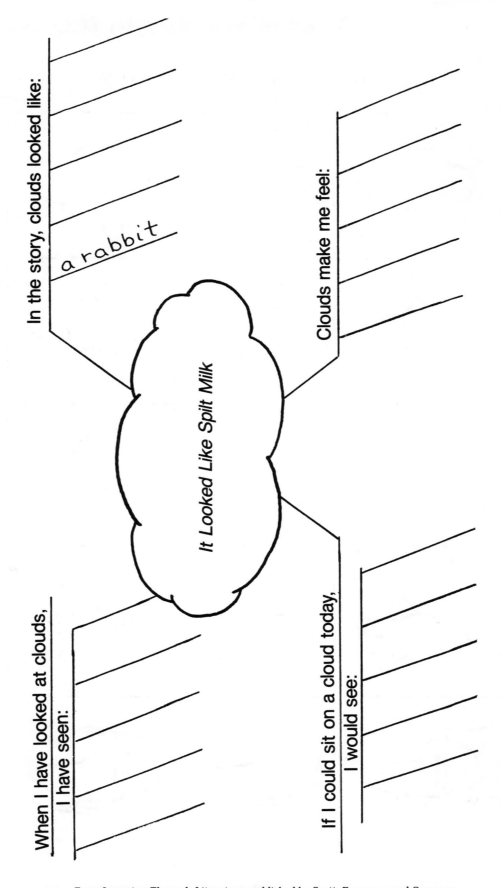

In the story, clouds looked like:

a rabbit

It Looked Like Spilt Milk

Clouds make me feel:

When I have looked at clouds, I have seen:

If I could sit on a cloud today, I would see:

Things We See in the Sky

Put an X on the picture in each row that is different.

Clouds and Raindrops

WINTER

The Snowy Day, Ezra Jack Keats, The Viking Press, 1962.
A small boy uses his imagination to amuse himself
outdoors on a snowy day. This Caldecott Award book is as
quiet and as beautiful as the falling snow.

Introductory Activity

Surprise Box   Put a real snowball in the surprise box.

Art Activities

**Soap-Painted
Snowmen**   Make soap paint by mixing two cups of powdered detergent
with lukewarm water. Add the water gradually and mix to
the consistency of whipped cream. (Makes enough for 12
children.) The children can use the soap paint like
fingerpaint.

          To paint a snowman, the children spread soap paint on
blue construction paper. You can either draw circles on the
paper for the children to fill in or allow them to create free-
form snowmen. You may want to have the children add
hats, scarves, buttons, and facial features. Construction
paper scraps, buttons, and fabrics will stick if pressed into
the soap-painted picture while it is still wet.

*Snowman Face   Trace a 6-inch circle on a 9x12-inch sheet of construction
paper and have the children fill it in with soap paint. Have
the children add the black top hat, carrot nose, and
knotted scarf from the worksheet. They can use the black
dots for eyes and a mouth. Or they can substitute a fabric
scarf and real buttons for the eyes.

---

*Indicates activity that has an accompanying reproducible worksheet.

Molded Snowman

Mix two cups of sawdust, one cup of wheatpaste, and enough water to make a dough of modeling consistency. Have the children mold the dough into snowballs, connecting two or three balls to form a snowman. Let the dough dry for 24-48 hours before painting with white tempera and adding facial features and decorations.

Paper Ring Snowman

Cut strips of white paper—2½x7 inches, 3x9 inches, and 3½x11 inches. Overlap the ends of each strip and paste to form circles. Fasten the circles together with the largest on bottom and the smallest on top. Decorate with snowman accessories.

Cavalcade of Snowmen

There are many other ways to make snowmen. You can make them out of paper plates, doilies, and cotton balls as well as white construction paper. Decorate with buttons, yarn, fabric, etc.

Snow Angels

Lay white chalk lengthwise on a piece of dark construction paper and twist to make an angel shape. You can make the angel's head by twisting the chalk in a circle on its writing tip.

Spatter-Painted Snowflakes

For this activity you will need an old window screen, toothbrushes, and a plastic tub. Start by cutting a large variety of paper snowflakes. Let each child choose two or three snowflakes and arrange them on a piece of construction paper in the tub. After placing the screen over the tub, the child dips a toothbrush into thinned paint and rubs it over the screen so that the paint spatters on the paper (hint: too much paint will make blobs on the paper). You may want to try blue paint on white paper or white paint on dark paper. When the child is finished painting, remove the snowflakes from the paper. Isn't it beautiful?

Indicates activity that has an accompanying reproducible worksheet.

Snowflake Prints   Obtain a rosette iron—available in the housewares section of most department stores—and let the children dip it in white paint and stamp it onto blue paper to make snowflake-shaped prints.

*Sled   Reproduce the worksheet on tagboard or construction paper. Let the children cut out and assemble the sled and then decorate it with paint, crayons, or stamp designs.

Winter Mural   Have the children sketch pictures of themselves engaged in their favorite winter activities. Encourage them to decorate their self-portraits with yarn, fabric, foil, and paper. The children may also enjoy sketching trees and using yarn to fill in the shape. When all the figures and shapes are finished and dry, the children can cut them out and arrange them into a mural on a bulletin board.

Language Development

Words to Grow By

pretended	handful
mountain climber	adventures
heaping	

Something to Think About   What are some of the things Peter did in the snow?
Why did Peter's snowball melt?
How can you keep a snowball in your house?
What do you like to do in the snow?

Winter Words   Challenge the children to think of as many words as they can that pertain to winter. Have older children try to use all of the words in a story. Younger children can dictate their ideas to an adult.

---

*Indicates activity that has an accompanying reproducible worksheet.

*Sequence

Duplicate, laminate, and then cut apart the "Building a Snowman" and "The Snowman and the Sunny Day" worksheets. Talk about the correct sequence, then scramble the pictures, and set them out as a table game. Or you can make copies of the worksheet for each child to cut apart and then paste in the correct sequence on 6x18-inch strips of paper.

Creative Dramatics

The Snowy Day is a good story for children to act out. They will enjoy making tracks like Peter, forming snow angels, and throwing snowballs.

Winter Riddles

You can help the children develop receptive language skills by giving them clues that describe winter-related items. Encourage older children to print the riddles for writing practice and to draw pictures of the clues as a comprehension exercise.

> You wear them on your hands. (mittens or gloves)
> It keeps your neck warm. (scarf)
> They keep your feet dry. (boots)
> Put these on your ears. (earmuffs)
> This will keep your head warm. (hat)
> Use this to dig a path through the snow. (shovel)

*What's Wrong with Winter?

Give each child a copy of the worksheet and ask them to point out and describe everything that is wrong with the picture. This activity challenges children to apply what they know about seasons, appropriate clothing, and activities. In addition to exercising visual discrimination, the children must also use language skills in describing what's wrong.

Fine and Gross Motor Skills _____

*The Snowman and the Bunny

To finish the pictures of the snowman and the bunny, children will need to use their problem-solving, visual, and motor skills.

---

*Indicates activity that has an accompanying reproducible worksheet.

*Snowman Match   Make a copy of this visual discrimination activity for each child. Have the children draw lines linking identical snowman faces.

Snowflake Match   Cut snowflakes out of two pieces of layered tissue paper so that you have identical pairs. Make several such pairs, mount each on posterboard, and laminate. Then challenge the children to match the identical snowflakes. You can make the matching easier by mounting one of each pair on blue posterboard and the other set on posterboard of another color.

Indoor Snow Fun   Fill a dishpan with snow and bring it inside. Let the children play with snow in the classroom.

Snowball Pick-Up   Let the children pick up cotton balls with tongs and transfer them from one bowl to another.

Making Paper Snowballs   Have the children crumple up pieces of white paper and throw them at each other or at a target.

Snowman Target   Make a large snowman out of paper or posterboard. Hang the snowman from the lighting fixtures or ceiling, and let the children throw paper snowballs or Styrofoam balls at the target.

Snow Acts   The children can pretend to get dressed for outdoors to shovel, to ice skate, etc.

Snow Pantomimes   In this charades game, the children perform "Snow Acts" as pantomime for the others to guess. Younger children may need suggestions for their performances; whisper to them, "Pretend you're putting on boots (a scarf, etc.)." Older children can think up their own snow acts.

Indicates activity that has an accompanying reproducible worksheet.

From *Learning Through Literature*, published by Scott, Foresman and Company.
Copyright © 1991 Mary Jane Butner, Jane Ann Peterson, and Janice Marks Sieplinga.

Balance   Challenge the children to stand on one foot and use their other foot to draw a snowman in the air.

Fingerplays and Songs

A Snowman
by Jane Peterson
(Tune: "One Bottle of Pop" Camp Song)

Part 1:

One ball of snow, two balls of snow, three balls of snow, a snowman.

One ball of snow, two balls of snow, three balls of snow, a snow–man.

Part 2:

But–ton eyes and car–rot nose, car–rot nose, car–rot nose,

But–ton eyes and car–rot nose, and a stove–pipe hat.

Part 3:

Here comes a lit–tle rab–bit, rab–bit, rab–bit,

Here comes a lit–tle rab–bit, look–ing for his lunch.

Here comes a lit–tle rab–bit, rab–bit, rab–bit,

Here comes a lit–tle rab–bit, nib–ble, nib–ble, nib–ble, crunch!

Indicates activity that has an accompanying reproducible worksheet.

Snowman Counting Rhyme
by Mary Jane Butner

One little snowman has a carrot nose.
Two snowmen shiver when the cold wind blows.
Three little snowmen wear scarves when it snows.
Four little snowmen are getting cold toes.
Five little snowmen like to pose
Outside—night and day—in their winter clothes.

Cooking

Snow Cones   Put crushed ice in paper cups and top with flavored syrup.

Hot Chocolate   Let the children count out spoonfuls of hot chocolate mix in cups. Older children can then pour in hot water, but an adult should do the pouring for younger children. All can carefully stir their hot chocolate until it is cool enough to drink.

Science

Snowball Science   Bring a snowball into the classroom and have the children observe it as it melts. Have them note the dirt particles in the snow.

Indicates activity that has an accompanying reproducible worksheet.

Snow Experiments   Ask the children some snow-related questions. Should you eat snow? How could you keep a snowball from melting inside? Near heat? Far from heat? In a plastic bag? In a paper bag? In a covered plastic bowl? How could you make a snowball melt faster? Where does snow melt first outside? (On salted streets and sidewalks)

Have the children do an experiment in the classroom by placing two ice cubes in a dish, putting rock salt on one of them, and noting which ice cube melts first.

Snowflakes   Go outside on a snowy day and catch some snowflakes on black construction paper. Have the children use a magnifying glass to observe the flakes.

Snow Walk   Take the children outdoors when there is snow on the ground. Look for bird and other animal tracks in the snow. Make some tracks or use a stick to make some other markings in the snow.

Math

Seriation   Put out several construction paper snowballs in a variety of sizes. Have the children put the snowballs in order from largest to smallest.

Graph Questions   Make a graph based on one of the following questions. Have the children check the appropriate column (yes or no). Then have them count the answers and compare the columns.

Do you have mittens or gloves?
Did you wear a scarf today?
Do you like to play in the snow?

Indicates activity that has an accompanying reproducible worksheet.

Extended Experiences ————————————————

Coasting   Arrange to meet the children and their parents at a sliding hill. The children should bring their own sleds. Return to school afterwards for hot chocolate.

Field Trips   Take the children to visit a nature center during winter or to a skating rink.

Related Books ————————————————

All of these books provide enjoyable reading experiences about winter fun:

Snow, Kathleen Todd, Addison-Wesley, 1982.

The Snow Baby, Margaret Hillert, Modern Curriculum Press, 1969.

Snow Birthday, Helen Kay, Farrar, Straus, and Giroux, 1955.

A Winter Day, Douglas Florian, Greenwillow Books, 1987.

A Winter Friend, Maxine W. Kumin, G. P. Putnam's Sons, 1961.

A Winter Place, Ruth Yaffe Radin, Little Brown and Company, 1982.

Indicates activity that has an accompanying reproducible worksheet.

Snowman Face

Sled

*paper fastener

x tie with yarn

handle

(Due to page size limitations, this pattern had to be reduced. Teachers— especially those working with younger children—may want to enlarge the pattern before reproducing and distributing it.)

Sequence: Building a Snowman

Sequence:
The Snowman and the Sunny Day

What's Wrong with Winter?

The Snowman and the Bunny

Finish the bunny and the snowman.

Snowman Match

SPRING

A Rainbow of My Own, Don Freeman, Viking Press, 1966.
What fun to have a rainbow of your very own!

Introductory Activities

Surprise Box

Put a prism or some color paddles in the surprise box.

ROY G. BIV

Introduce the children to ROY G. BIV to help them remember the order of colors in a rainbow: **R**ed, **O**range, **Y**ellow, **G**reen, **B**lue, **I**ndigo, **V**iolet.

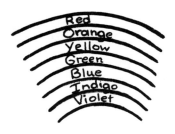

Rainbow Visual Aid

Use colored posterboard to make arcs in graduated sizes corresponding to the order of colors in the rainbow—with red as the largest arc and violet as the smallest. Laminate the arcs, stack one on top of the other to form a rainbow, and link them together with ring fasteners.

Indicates activity that has an accompanying reproducible worksheet.

Art Activities

Crepe Paper Rainbow

Wet one side of a piece of white drawing paper. Lay torn pieces of colored crepe paper on the wet side of the drawing paper. Now wet another piece of drawing paper and lay it—wet side down—on the first sheet so that the crepe paper is sandwiched in between. Let the paper sandwich dry and then pull the two sheets of drawing paper apart. Throw away the used crepe paper. You will have multicolored pieces of drawing paper that you can then cut into a rainbow shape.

Tear Paper Rainbow

Tear rainbow-colored pieces of construction paper and paste on an arc-shaped piece of paper.

Crayon Shavings Rainbow

Use a pencil sharpener or vegetable grater to make a pile of crayon shavings. Place the shavings between sheets of wax paper, cover with a piece of paper or cloth, and then iron. The crayon shavings will melt and blend together. Cut the wax paper in a rainbow shape when it has cooled.

Yarn Rainbow

Glue yarn in a rainbow shape.

Paint a Rainbow

Have the children use fingerpaints, watercolors, or tempera paint to paint a rainbow.

Color a Rainbow

Using the sides of crayons or colored chalk, trace a series of arcs on paper. To give the rainbow a translucent look, rub cooking oil on the back of the paper.

*Indicates activity that has an accompanying reproducible worksheet.

Language Development _____

Words to Grow By   While the vocabulary in *A Rainbow of My Own* is
                         minimal, you may want to introduce some of the following
                         words when discussing the story:

prism	primary colors
spectrum	secondary colors
arc	tints
color wheel	indigo

Something to   What are all the places where the boy saw a rainbow?
Think About   How did the boy get to have a "real" rainbow of his own?
                         If you could have a rainbow, what would you do with it?
                         Could you really play with a rainbow?
                         Have you ever seen a rainbow?
                         Where did you see a rainbow?
                         When do rainbows appear?

*Chasing   Do this story map as a group activity with younger
Rainbows   children. Make a copy for each older child to do
                         independently.

Guess Who   Give color clues to identify a specific child in the class—
                         e.g., "I'm thinking of a girl who is wearing a purple dress,"
                         or ". . . a boy with blue shoes." This activity challenges the
                         children to use receptive language skills.

Creative Writing   Have the children make up stories that start "I followed
                         the rainbow to its end and I found . . . ." Older children
                         can write their stories; younger children can dictate their
                         stories to an adult.

*What's Wrong   Give each child a copy of the worksheet. Ask the children
with Springtime?   to find the eight things wrong in the picture. This activity
                         challenges the children's thinking, visual discrimination,
                         and language skills.

_____

*Indicates activity that has an accompanying reproducible worksheet.

Fine and Gross Motor Skills _____

*A Color Surprise   This activity promotes visual discrimination and fine motor skills while developing letter and color recognition.

*Ice Cream Cones   Use a wide variety of colors for the ice cream scoops and drips. Glue a drip of ice cream on the rim of the cone and print the name of the color in the drip. Then have the children match the color of the ice cream in the scoop to the color of the ice cream drip on the cone.

Color-Shape Bingo   Play this commercially available game with the children.

Pegs, Beads   String beads or arrange pegs in the pegboard so that they appear in the same order as the colors of the rainbow (ROY G BIV).

Crepe Streamers   Using crepe paper in rainbow colors, give each child a crepe streamer. Let the children run around with the paper streaming behind them, twirl the paper in circles or other shapes, jump over the streamers, or move them in time to music.

Rainbow Twister   Play the commercially available Twister game according to the rules or adapt the game to the needs of younger children.

Musical Colors   Using a variety of colors and allowing at least one sheet of paper per child, arrange 9x12-inch sheets of construction paper in a circle. Have the children march around the circle in time to music. Tell them that when the music stops each is to pick up a nearby piece of paper. Then have each child identify the color of the paper he is holding. Repeat the activity several times so that all the children get to identify several colors.

_____

Indicates activity that has an accompanying reproducible worksheet.

From *Learning Through Literature*, published by Scott, Foresman and Company.
Copyright © 1991 Mary Jane Butner, Jane Ann Peterson, and Janice Marks Sieplinga.

Fingerplays and Songs

Share a Rainbow
by Mary Jane Butner, Jane Peterson, Janice Marks Sieplinga

It's raining, it's raining—
The sunlight shines through,
Painting a rainbow
Especially for you.

The colors are lovely;
They make you feel glad.
You feel you must share it
With Mother and Dad.

Rainbow Nonsense
by ROY G. BIV

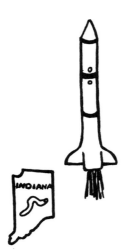

Red rockets rise rapidly.
Orange ogres ooze oleo.
Yellow yo-yos yerk and yump
(And that's no yoke, by yimminy!)
Green gorillas glide gracefully on grass.
Blue blennies blow blue bubbles.
Indigo inchworms invade Indiana.
Violet vipers visit violent vultures.

*(Children will enjoy illustrating these silly tongue twisters, and
they may want to create their own alliterative nonsense.)*

---

*Indicates activity that has an accompanying reproducible worksheet.

Rainbow Colors
by Mary Jane Butner
(Tune: "Twinkle, Twinkle, Little Star")

Rainbow, rainbow, shining so,
Tell me how your colors go.
Red, orange, yellow, green, and blue.
Indigo and violet too.
Rainbow, rainbow, way up high.
Shimmering lightly in the sky.

I Saw a Rainbow
by Mary Jane Butner, Jane Peterson, Janice Marks Sieplinga
(Tune: "I Saw Three Ships" Traditional English Carol)

I saw a rain–bow in the sky, While rain–drops fell the sun came through.

I saw a rain–bow in the sky, And now the col–ors I'll tell you.

There's red, orange, yel–low, green, and blue, And in–di–go, vio–let—

the col–ors true. I saw a rain–bow in the sky,

When sun rays peeked through the rain–drops.

*Indicates activity that has an accompanying reproducible worksheet.

Cooking

Rainbow Treat

You can prepare the following recipe on a hotplate in the classroom. Start by melting a 12-ounce package of chocolate chips and a stick of butter. Allow to cool to room temperature and then stir in 1 Tbsp. of water, 1 tsp. of vanilla, and a 10½-ounce package of miniature colored marshmallows. Form into two rolls (optional: roll in coconut); wrap in wax paper. Refrigerate until firm, cut into slices, and then cut each slice in half to form a rainbow arc.

Science

Make a Prism

Fill a transparent plastic shoebox or a clear-glass loaf pan with water. Place the water-filled container on a table where it will catch the sun's rays. Try moving a mirror along the side of the box or pan so that the light passing through the water reflects on the mirror.

Prism Projections

Hang some prisms (available through school catalogs) in the classroom windows. The children will be delighted to see rainbows projected on the floor, walls, and ceiling!

Bubbles

Make a bubble solution by mixing 1/4 cup liquid detergent, 2 quarts water, and 1/4 cup sugar. After cautioning them to blow rather than inhale, give each child a straw and a cup of the bubble solution. Encourage the children to make pretty "bubble sculptures," and share their delight in watching bubbles overflow the sides of the cups. Also have the children note the colors in the bubbles and ask them to guess how the colors got there.

Since this is a messy activity, you might be well advised to wait for a sunny day and do it outside.

Indicates activity that has an accompanying reproducible worksheet.

Crystals

To make delicate, colorful crystals in the classroom, lay pieces of charcoal in a shallow container and pour a mixture of 1/4 cup salt (noniodized), 1/4 cup bluing, 1/4 cup water, and 1/4 cup ammonia over them. The crystals will begin to form in a day or two. Add more of the mixture every two days to keep them growing. To make more colorful crystals, add some food coloring to the mixture.

Color Mixing

Let the children experiment with mixing primary colors to make other colors.

*Color Glasses

Use the pattern to make three pairs of glasses out of tagboard. Glue in "lenses" of red cellophane in one pair, yellow cellophane in the second, and blue cellophane in the third pair. If cellophane is not available, color some plastic wrap or overhead projector transparencies with red, yellow, and blue markers. Punch a hole in each pair of glasses and join the three together with a paper fastener. Have the children look through any two pairs at one time to see how two primary colors mix to create a new color.

Color Experiments

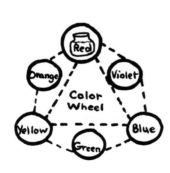

Gather six baby food jars and add water and food coloring to three of the jars: one red, one blue, and one yellow. Then pour from these jars into the empty jars to demonstrate how primary colors can be mixed to create secondary colors. Mix red and yellow in one jar, red and blue in another, and blue and yellow in the last jar. Have the children identify the new colors formed. You can use all six jars to make a color wheel.

Indicates activity that has an accompanying reproducible worksheet.

Math ─────────────────────────────

Graph

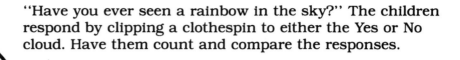

"Have you ever seen a rainbow in the sky?" The children respond by clipping a clothespin to either the Yes or No cloud. Have them count and compare the responses.

Extended Experiences ─────────────

Field Trip   Take the children to visit an art gallery.

Resource Person   Invite an artist—painter, weaver, etc.—to the class.

Related Books ─────────────────────

The Color Kittens, Margaret Wise Brown, Golden Press, 1977.
  Brush and Hush experiment with their paint cans to make beautiful new colors.

Paddington and the Knickerbocker Rainbow, Michael Bond and David McKee, G. P. Putnam's Sons, 1985.
  Paddington enjoys a visit to the seashore.

What Color Is It? Elizabeth Ivanovsky, Derrydale Books, Crown Publishers, 1986.
  This book introduces primary colors and shows how they can be combined to make secondary colors and tints.

*Indicates activity that has an accompanying reproducible worksheet.

Chasing Rainbows

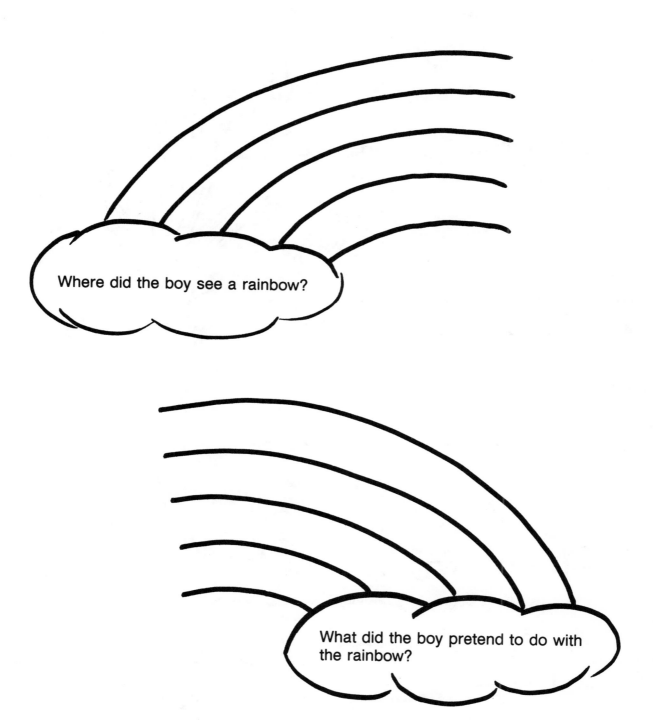

Where did the boy see a rainbow?

What did the boy pretend to do with the rainbow?

What's Wrong with Springtime?

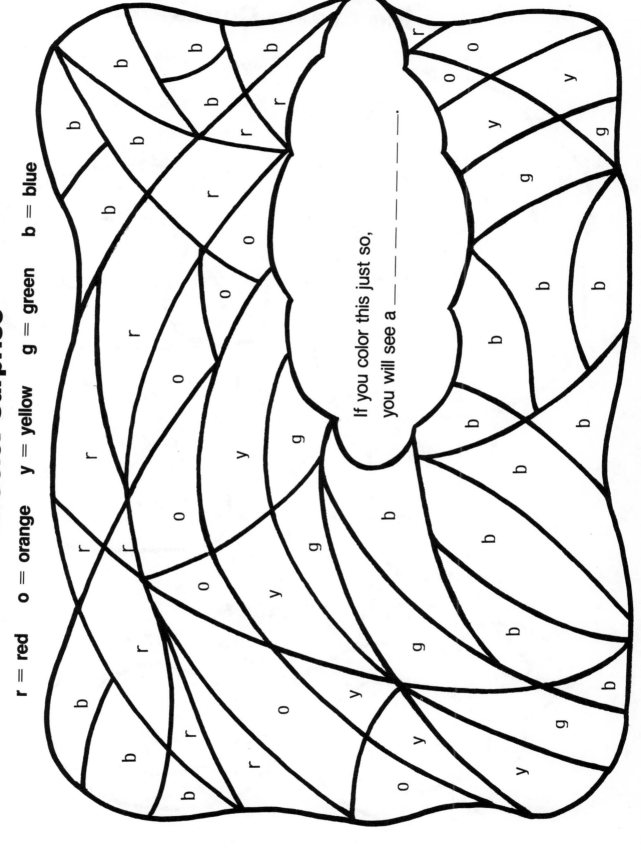

Ice Cream Cones

cut on dots

red

Color Glasses

From *Learning Through Literature*, published by Scott, Foresman and Company.
Copyright © 1991 Mary Jane Butner, Jane Ann Peterson, and Janice Marks Sieplinga.

TRANSPORTATION

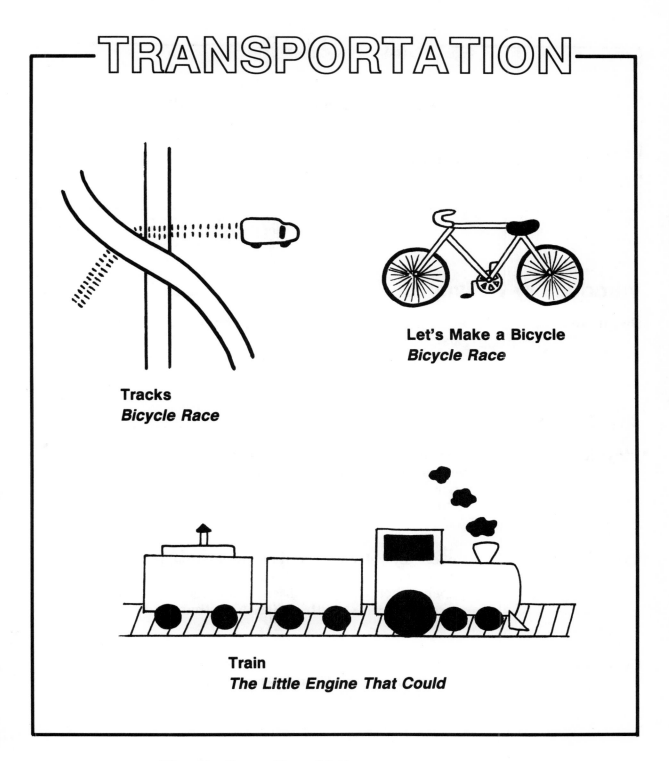

Tracks
Bicycle Race

Let's Make a Bicycle
Bicycle Race

Train
The Little Engine That Could

Bicycle Race, Donald Crews
The Little Engine That Could, Watty Piper

BICYCLES

Bicycle Race, Donald Crews, Greenwillow Books, 1985.
Who will win the bicycle race? The children have many
opportunities to identify numbers and colors before the
race is won by bicycle number . . .?

Introductory Activity

Surprise Box   Put a bicycle pedal, handle grip, or gear in the surprise
                          box.

Art Activities

*Bicycle   Reproduce copies of the bicycle frame and wheel
                          worksheets for each child. Have the children draw in
                          spokes and then cut out the wheels and attach them to the
                          frame with paper fasteners so that they are movable.

Tracks   Collect toy vehicles that have interesting, textured tires.
                          Let the children roll the toys through paint and then onto
                          paper. When the paint dries, challenge the children to
                          match the tracks with the vehicles that made them.

Color Fun   Point out to the children the twelve different shades of
                          color in the story. Then let them experiment with paints,
                          mixing them to create new shades of color.

*Indicates activity that has an accompanying reproducible worksheet.

Language Development

Words to Grow By While the vocabulary in *Bicycle Race* is minimal, you may want to introduce some of the following words when discussing the story in class:

bicycle	fastest
bike	speed
tricycle	helmet
unicycle	gears
ahead	brakes
behind	pedals
fast	chain
faster	

Something to Think About
Whom did you want to win the race?
Who won the race?
What happened to bike number nine?
Who do you think worked hardest in the bike race?

Bikes and Trikes Challenge the children to think of ways in which bicycles and tricycles are alike and ways in which they are different. Record the answers of younger children on chart paper. Older children can write their own lists.

Writing Have the children pretend to be sports reporters describing what they saw happen in the bicycle race.

Fine and Gross Motor Skills

*How Many Wheels? Make a copy of this counting and number-recognition matching activity for each child in the class.

*Bicycle Race Maze This worksheet can help children develop tracking, small muscle control, and decision-making skills.

*Indicates activity that has an accompanying reproducible worksheet.

Color Matching   Get paint sample cards—several for each color range—from a paint store and cut them up. Let the children match pieces from the same color card or arrange pieces from the lightest to the darkest shade of each color. This activity helps develop visual discrimination and seriation abilities.

*Bikes Alike!   Reproduce the helmet and shirt patterns, using the colors from *Bicycle Race.* Do the same with the bicycle pattern from "Bicycle," being sure to add wheels before reproducing. Cut out and laminate all the helmets, shirts, and bikes to use as a table game. The children can group together all the bikes, all the helmets, all the shirts; or they can group together all the items of the same color.

Making Roads   Give the children large sheets of paper and markers and have them draw roads. You can also encourage them to draw roads on the chalkboard or build roads with blocks. Challenge them to add bridges to their roads and to make their roads go up and down hills.

Balance   Point out that riding a bike requires balance. Have the children perform a variety of balancing activities—walking on the balance beam, standing on one foot, hopping on one foot, etc.

Tricycle Relay   If tricycles are not part of your physical education equipment, see if you can borrow some. Then conduct a relay race in the gym or outside.

Pedal the Bike   Have the children lie on their backs with their feet in the air and make pedaling motions with their legs. Start them going slowly and then pick up the pace; also have them pretend to pedal uphill and downhill.

---

*Indicates activity that has an accompanying reproducible worksheet.

Fingerplays and Songs

A Wheel Silly Poem
by Mary Jane Butner

If there's one wheel on a unicycle;
And two wheels on a bicycle;
And three wheels on a tricycle;
How many wheels on an icicle?

Color Bikes
by Mary Jane Butner

I go uphill and then I go down
When I ride my bike of _____ . (brown)

I go to the store to buy some bread.
I get there on my bike of _____ . (red)

I rode so fast I lost my shoe.
My bike is fast; my bike is _____ .

I have the prettiest bike you've ever seen;
It's shiny and new and it is _____ .

I'd never go near the railroad track;
A train might smash my bike of _____ .

Today is my birthday and what do you think?
I got a new bike and it is _____ .

Do You Have a Bike?
by Mary Jane Butner
(Tune: "Do Your Ears Hang Low?")

Do you have a bike? Is it one you really like?
Can you go as fast as Pat? Can you go as fast as Mike?
Do you like it better than you liked your little trike?
Do you have a bike?

Yes, I have a bike; yes, it's one I really like.
I can go as fast as Pat; I can go as fast as Mike.
Yes, I like it better than I liked my little trike.
Yes, I have a bike.

Indicates activity that has an accompanying reproducible worksheet.

From *Learning Through Literature,* published by Scott, Foresman and Company.
Copyright © 1991 Mary Jane Butner, Jane Ann Peterson, and Janice Marks Sieplinga.

Cooking ———————————————————

Hot Wheels

In a large bowl dissolve a package of yeast in 1½ cups warm water. Add 1 tsp. salt and 1 Tbsp. sugar, blend in 4 cups of flour, and knead. Give each child a piece of dough and show the children how to roll the dough into ropes and then into a circle. They can crisscross other pieces of dough to form spokes on their wheels. Place the dough circles on a lightly greased cookie sheet, brush with a beaten egg, and sprinkle with coarse salt. Bake at 425° for 12-15 minutes. The pretzels are best when eaten warm—"hot wheels"!

Science ———————————————————

Wheels, Wheels Everywhere!

Challenge the children to think of all the things a wheel can do, all the places they see wheels, and all the different kinds of wheels there are. Discuss how gears affect wheels. Put out items with gears—egg beater, hand drill, sand mill, toy cement mixer, etc.—for the children to examine.

Old and New Bikes

Display pictures of both antique and modern bikes. Ask the children how the old and new bikes are alike. How are they different?

Math ———————————————————

Graph

Bicycle	Bike 4 wheels	Tricycle
Dana Matt	Bryna Kim	Todd Aimee

Make a graph with these headings: Bicycle, Bicycle with Training Wheels, Tricycle. Have the children mark the appropriate column for the kind of bike they have. Then have them count and compare the totals for the three columns.

———————————————————————————

*Indicates activity that has an accompanying reproducible worksheet.

Bike Race   Make a series of color cards and another series of cards with numbers. Line up the children at a starting line and give each child a different colored placard to wear (the colors corresponding to the color cards). Hold up one of the color cards and one of the number cards. The child wearing that color placard then takes the number of steps shown on the number card. The child who crosses the pre-determined finish line first wins the race.

Extended Experiences _____

Resource Person   Invite a police officer to talk to the children about bicycle safety.

Follow the Signs   Set up "roads" and miniature traffic signs in the school parking lot. Have the children ride their bicycles or tricycles around the lot, obeying the posted signs.

Related Books _____

Bears on Wheels, Stan and Jan Berenstain, Random House, 1969.
 In this counting book the bears ride some very strange cycles—with one, two, three, four, and five wheels.

The Bike Lesson, Stan and Jan Berenstain, Random House, 1964.
 Here's how *not* to ride a bike, in seven easy lessons.

Shawn's Red Bike, Petronella Breinburg, Thomas V. Crowell Company, 1976.
 Shawn saves to get a big, new, two-wheel bike; the next step—learn to ride it!

*Indicates activity that has an accompanying reproducible worksheet.

Bicycle

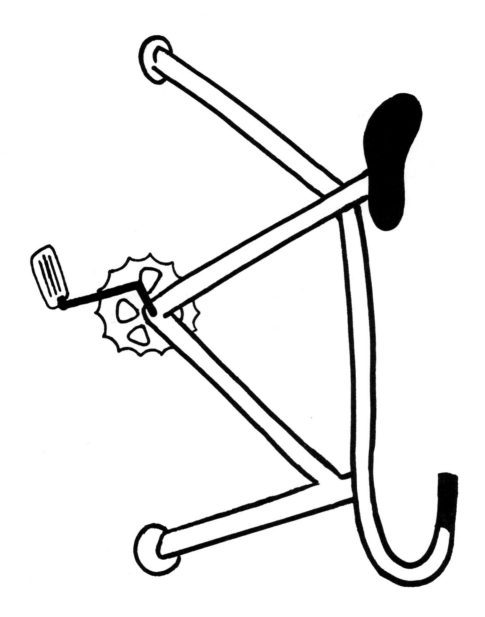

Bicycle

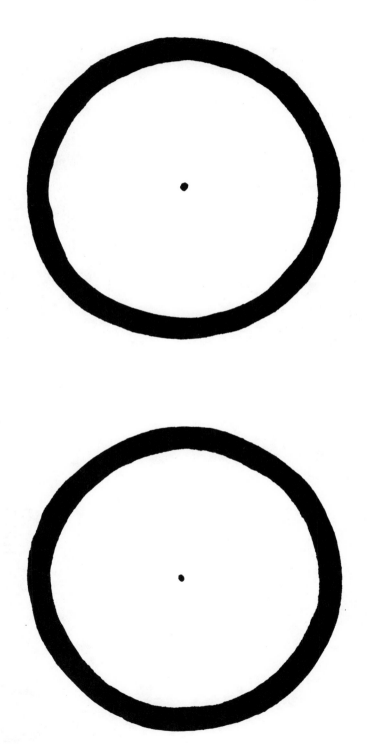

How Many Wheels?

1

2

3

4

Bicycle Race Maze

Ride the bike down the path to the winner's flag.

Bikes Alike!

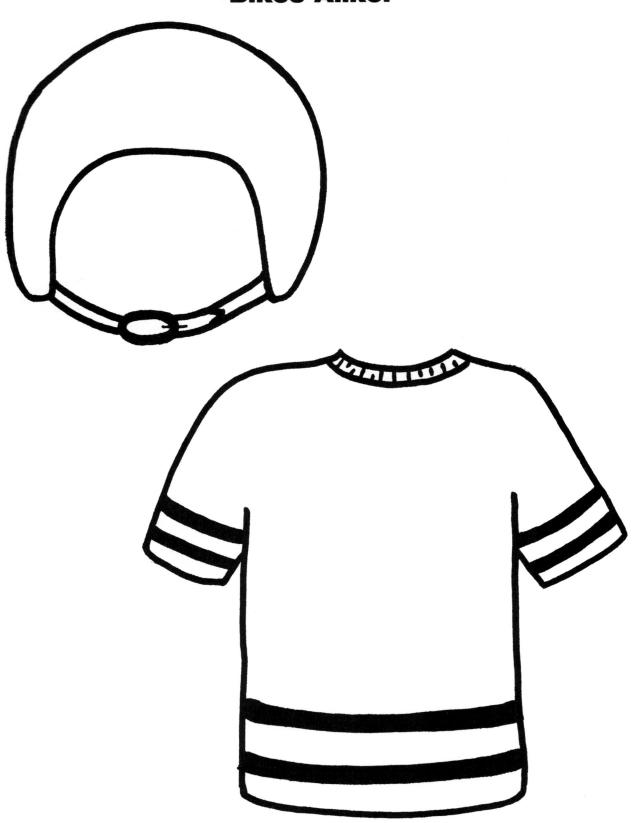

```
┌─────────────────────────────────────────────────────────────────┐
│                        ┌─ TRAINS ─┐                               │
│                                                                   │
│   The Little Engine That Could, Watty Piper, Platt & Munk, 1961.  │
│     The little blue engine kindly agrees to pull the train over   │
│     the mountain. She thought she could, she thought she could—   │
│     and she did!                                                  │
│                                                                   │
└─────────────────────────────────────────────────────────────────┘
```

Introductory Activity

Surprise Box   Put a toy locomotive in the surprise box to initiate a discussion of trains.

Art Activities

*Little Engine That Could   Reproduce the patterns on the worksheets, using blue paper for the engine, red for the caboose, and some other color for the boxcar. Let the children cut out the cars and paste them on 12x18-inch sheets of construction paper. If they like, the children can add train tracks, smoke from the smokestack, and goods in the boxcar.

*Shape Engine   Have the children identify and color the shapes that make up the shape engine.

---

*Indicates activity that has an accompanying reproducible worksheet.

*Number Train   Reproduce the worksheet from the "Little Engine That Could" activity. You may want to make several boxcars for each child. Make each car a different color and put a number on each. Older children can paste the cars in order on construction paper. For younger children, print corresponding numbers on sheets of 12x18-inch construction paper. Have the children paste the train cars on the correct numbers. This requires the children to use visual discrimination skills.

3-D Train   Let the children experiment with a variety of boxes—milk cartons, shoe and food boxes, oatmeal containers—to construct a train. Give them heavy posterboard to make the wheels, and show them how to attach the wheels with paper fasteners or wood dowels. Display the finished train in the classroom.

Language Development

Words to Grow By

engine   freight
passenger   dingy
berth   locomotive
roundhouse   caboose

Something to Think About

Why was the little train going over the mountain?
What did the Little Blue Engine say as she pulled the
      train?
How could you be like the Little Engine if you're having
      trouble learning to do something?
What are some other ways that food and toys can be
      delivered?

*Indicates activity that has an accompanying reproducible worksheet.

From *Learning Through Literature*, published by Scott, Foresman and Company.

| **Transportation Riddles** | Find or draw pictures of a variety of vehicles and display the pictures in the classroom. Then give clues that identify the vehicles—e. g., "I'm thinking of something that goes in the water . . . in the air . . . that takes sick people to the hospital." The children must use receptive language skills to discover which vehicle is being described. |

| **Train Trip** | Have one child say, "I'm going on a train trip to . . . ," and then fill in a destination. The next child repeats what the first child said and adds a new destination. With very young children, have the whole group recite the list of places, and let the child whose turn it is merely add a new one. |

| ***Story Frame** | A story frame helps children recall details and identify the story's main idea. Not simply a fill-in-the-blanks activity, it requires the children to use writing skills. |

Fine and Gross Motor Skills _____

| **Classification Game** | Make several train cars and put a different picture on each—a fruit, a vegetable, a toy. Then find or draw other pictures that fit into the same categories (old workbooks are a good source). Have the children put each picture in the appropriate train car. |

| ***I Think I Can, I Think I Can!** | Reproduce the worksheet for each child. Tell the children to follow each set of tracks from the little engine to the mountain. This activity helps develop left to right readiness. |

| ***Color and Shape Train** | Make a copy of the worksheet for each child. Have the children color each shape on the train according to the color/shape code. |

Indicates activity that has an accompanying reproducible worksheet.

*Shape Train Puzzle

Cut two 7x22-inch strips of heavy white posterboard and tape them together to form one long 7x44-inch strip. Use the worksheet patterns to draw an outline of the shape train on the posterboard. Then use other colors of posterboard to make the various cars. Have the children lay the colored cars on the corresponding outlined shapes.

Number Train

Purchase an inexpensive plastic train. Number the cars, beginning with "1" for the engine. Have each child attach the other cars in numerical order.

The Train Game

Let the children form themselves into a train by holding onto each other's waist or by holding onto a rope. Put down a masking tape track for them to follow. Tell them when to go fast, slow, uphill (on tiptoe), and downhill (with bended knees). Have them chant "I think I can, I think I can."

The Long, Long Train

Make train car cutouts from several different colors of construction paper. Be sure to include an engine and a caboose. Laminate the cars and attach yarn so that the children can wear them around their necks. Then give directions—e. g., "Blue car, stand behind the engine. Yellow car, stand between the purple and green cars." Etc.

Fingerplays and Songs _____

Train Chant
by Mary Jane Butner

All aboard!   Toot-toot, toot-toot-toot
Choo-choo, choo-choo-choo   Ding-ding, ding-ding-ding
Chug-chug, chug-chug-chug   Sh-sh, sh-sh-sh
Puff-puff, puff-puff-puff   S-h-h-h-h-h-h-h!

(The children stand in a line, hands on shoulders of child in front, swaying rhythmically as they chant.)

---

*Indicates activity that has an accompanying reproducible worksheet.

Little Blue Engine
by Mary Jane Butner and Jane Peterson
(Tune: "Skip to My Lou" Traditional)

Slowly

Huff, puff, I think I can! Huff, puff, I think I can!

Huff, puff, I think I can! Get to the top of the mountain.

Little blue engine pulling toys, Games and treats for girls and boys.

Climbing slowly to the top, She's de - termined. She won't stop!

Faster

Toot! Toot! I thought I could! Toot! Toot! I thought I could!

Toot! Toot! I thought I could! Get to the top of the mountain.

Traditional *I've Been Working on the Railroad*
Down by the Station

Indicates activity that has an accompanying reproducible worksheet.

From *Learning Through Literature*, published by Scott, Foresman and Company.
Copyright © 1991 Mary Jane Butner, Jane Ann Peterson, and Janice Marks Sieplinga.

Cooking _____

The Little Engine That Could Be Eaten

Ingredients:

3-inch pieces of celery (several per child)
cream cheese or other spreadable cheese
"Bugles" corn snacks (one per child)
saltines (one per child)
sliced radishes, cucumbers, or zucchini

Have the children fill in the celery with cheese spread, add a "Bugle" for a smokestack, and a saltine for the cab of the engine. Then they can put small amounts of the cheese spread on the sliced vegetables and attach them to the celery as wheels. Let the children design other edible train cars to follow the engine.

Math _____

Train Ride Graph

Passenger Trains	Park Trains	Never
Glenn	Todd Dana	Keri

Make a picture graph of the children's train riding experiences. Ask the children the following questions:
    Who has ridden on a large passenger train?
    Who has ridden a train in an amusement park?
    Who has never ridden on any kind of train?

Extended Experiences _____

Field Trip

Take the children to visit a train station; if possible, take them on a short train ride.

Related Books _____

Freight Train, Donald Crews, Puffin Books, 1985.
    This Caldecott Honor Book has bright, colorful pictures showing the swift movement of a train.

Train Whistles, Helen Roney Sattler, Lothrop, Lee and Shepard, 1977.
    A colorful picture story about trains and the train whistle language.

*Indicates activity that has an accompanying reproducible worksheet.

Little Engine That Could

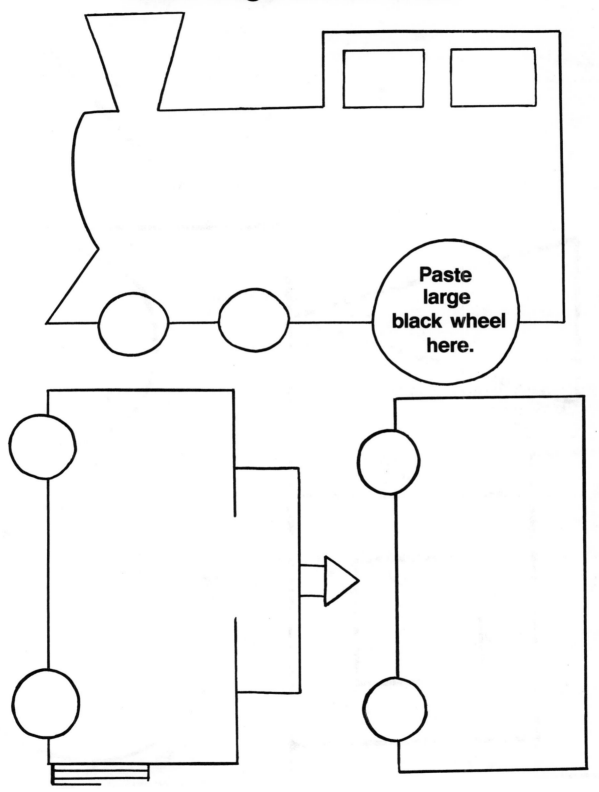

Paste large black wheel here.

Shape Engine

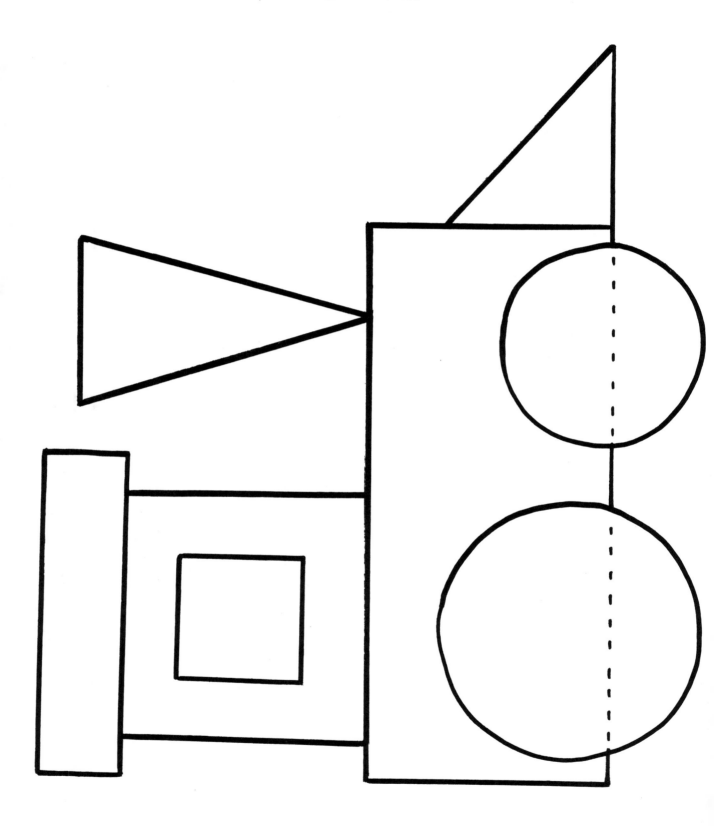

Story Frame:
The Little Engine That Could

A little train was _____

_____

_____

But suddenly she _____

_____

The toys and dolls wanted the shiny new engine to _____

_____

But the shiny new engine said, " _____

_____."

The big strong engine said, " _____

_____."

The rusty old engine said, " _____

_____."

The Little Blue Engine helped because _____

_____

_____

318

I Think I Can, I Think I Can!

Use a crayon to help each train reach the mountain.

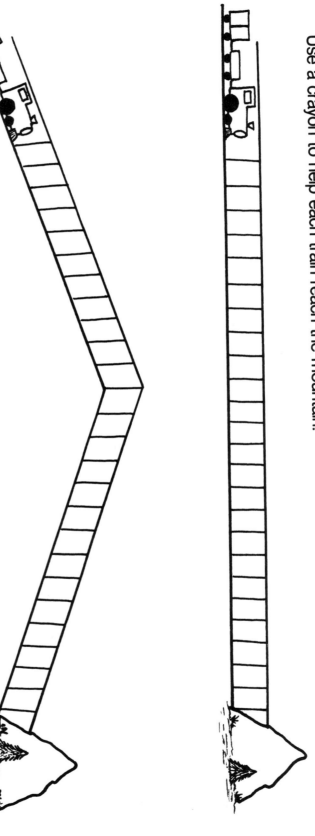

Name _____

Color and Shape Train

Read the color word. Then color the shapes.

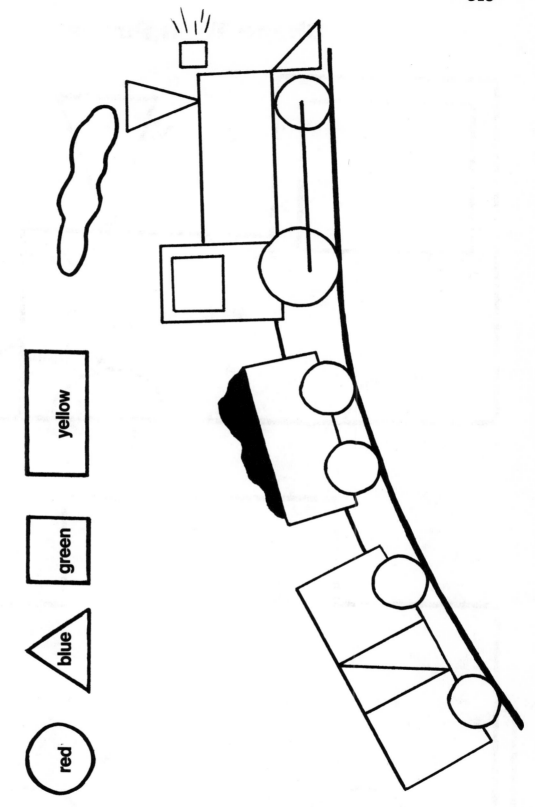

red

blue

green

yellow

Shape Train Puzzle

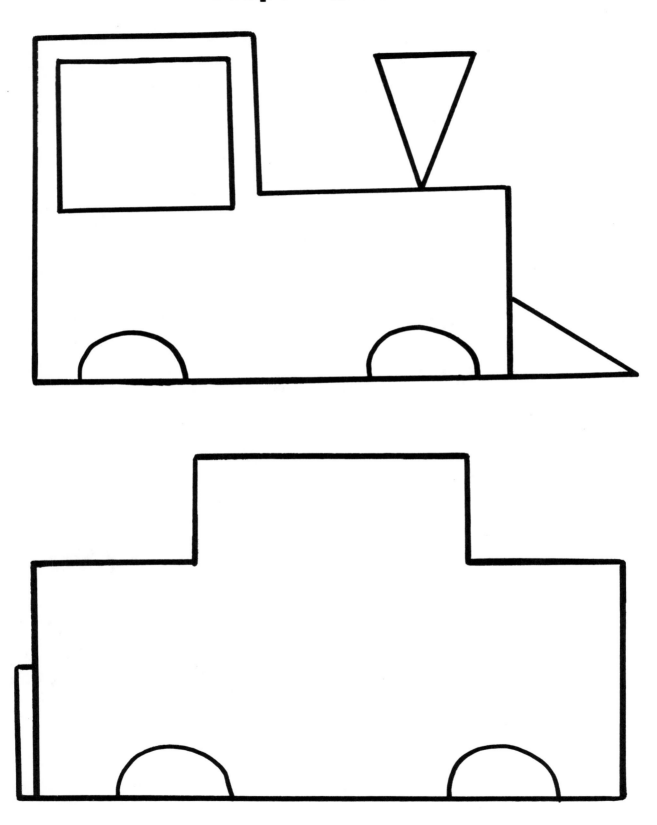

Shape Train Puzzle

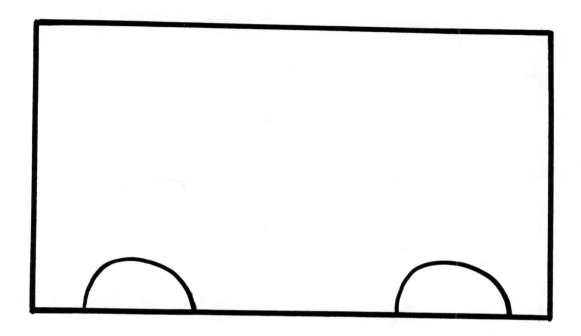

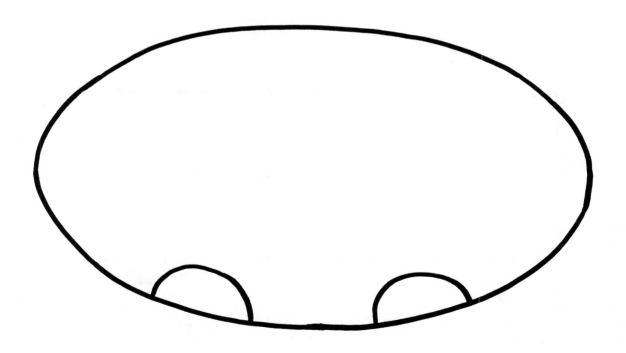

Shape Train Puzzle

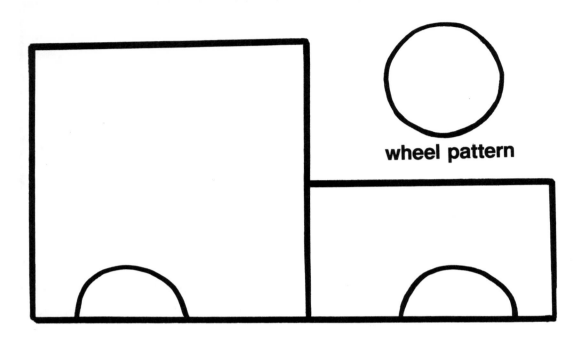

wheel pattern

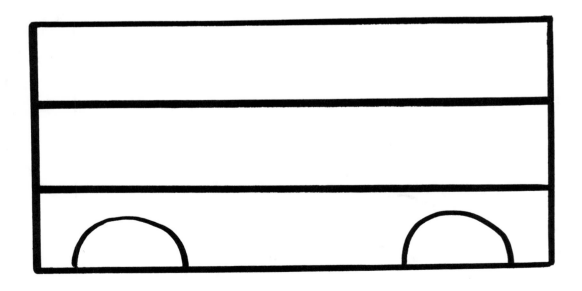

Index of Reproducible Worksheets

From *Learning Through Literature*, published by Scott, Foresman and Company.
Copyright © 1991 Mary Jane Butner, Jane Ann Peterson, and Janice Marks Sieplinga.

Mazes
> *Bicycle Race*
> *Curious George*
> *The Day of the Dinosaur*
> *Doctor DeSoto*
> *Make Way for Ducklings*
> *Six Foolish Fishermen*

Sequencing
> *Bread and Jam for Frances*
> *Little Red Hen*
> *Make Way for Ducklings*
> *The Snowy Day* (2 activities)

Seriation
> *The Great Big Fire Engine Book*
> *Little Red Hen*

Story Frames
> *Arthur's Eyes*
> *Bread and Jam for Frances*
> *Caps for Sale*
> *Corduroy*
> *Doctor DeSoto*
> *Frederick*
> *The Little Engine That Could*
> *Make Way for Ducklings*
> *Peter's Chair*

Story Maps
> *Clifford*
> *Curious George*
> *It Looked Like Spilt Milk*
> *Little Red Hen*
> *A Rainbow of My Own*
> *Six Foolish Fishermen*

Structured Story Starters
> *Clifford*
> *Curious George*
> *Stone Soup*

Visuals—Flannelboard Cutouts
> *The Day of the Dinosaur*
> *Doctor DeSoto* (2 activities)
> *Little Red Hen*
> *Make Way for Ducklings*
> *Stone Soup*

Visuals—Games
> *Bicycle Race*
> *Caps for Sale*
> *Clifford* (2 games)
> *Corduroy*
> *It looked Like Spilt Milk*
> *The Little Engine That Could*
> *Make Way for Ducklings*
> *A Rainbow of My Own* (2 games)
> *Six Foolish Fishermen*

What's Wrong with the Picture
> *A Rainbow of My Own*
> *The Snowy Day*

Word and Number Activities
> *The Day of the Dinosaur*
> *Frederick*
> *The Little Engine That Could*
> *Little Red Hen*
> *Make Way for Ducklings*
> *A Rainbow of My Own*
> *Stone Soup*

Alphabetical Listing
of Authors and Their Books

* Indicates main book title.

Years in parentheses following titles are copyright dates.

Bate, Lucy
  Little Rabbit's Loose Tooth (1975)

Berenstain, Stan and Jan
  Bears on Wheels (1969)
  The Bike Lesson (1964)
 * *The Day of the Dinosaur* (1987)
  Old Hat, New Hat (1970)

Bond, Michael
  *Paddington and the Knickerbocker
     Rainbow* (1985)

Breinburg, Petronella
  Shawn's Red Bike (1976)

Bridwell, Norman
 * *Clifford* (1972)
  Other books about Clifford

Brown, Marc
 * *Arthur's Eyes* (1973)
  Arthur's Tooth (1985)
  Other books about Arthur

Brown, Marcia
  Stone Soup (1947)

Brown, Margaret Wise
  The Color Kittens (1977)

Carrick, Carol
  Patrick's Dinosaurs (1983)

Clark, Mary Lou
  A New True Book of Dinosaurs
     (1955, 1981)

Cooney, Nancy Evans
  The Wobbly Tooth (1978)

Crews, Donald
 * *Bicycle Race* (1985)
  Freight Train (1985)

Daly, Kathleen N.
  Dinosaurs (1977)

de Paola, Tomie
  The Cloud Book (1975)

Elkin, Benjamin
 * *Six Foolish Fishermen* (1957)

Flack, Marjorie
  The Story About Ping (1933)

Florian, Douglas
  A Winter Day (1987)

Freeman, Don
  Beady Bear (1954)
  Bearymore (1976)
 * *Corduroy* (1968)
 * *A Pocket for Corduroy* (1978)
 * *A Rainbow of My Own* (1966)

Gibbons, Gail
   Fire! Fire! (1984)

Ginsburg, Mirra
   Good Morning, Chick (1980)

Gramatky, Hardie
   Hercules (1940)

Greenfield, Eloise
   She Come Bringing Me
   That Little Baby Girl (1974)

Hall, Bill
   Whatever Happens to Puppies (1965)

Heide, Florence Parry and
  Sylvia Worth Van Clief
   That's What Friends Are For (1968)

Hillert, Margaret
   The Snow Baby (1969)

Hitte, Kathryn
   Mexicali Soup (1970)

Hoban, Russell
   A Baby Sister for Frances (1964)
  * *Bread and Jam for Frances* (1974)
   Other stories about Frances

Hoban, Tana
   Look Again (1971)

Hoff, Syd
   Danny and the Dinosaur (1958)

Ivanovsky, Elizabeth
   What Color Is It? (1986)

Kay, Helen
   Snow Birthday (1955)

Keats, Ezra Jack
   Goggles (1969)
   Jenny's Hat (1966)
  * *Peter's Chair* (1967)
  * *The Snowy Day* (1962)

Kraus, Robert
   Big Brother (1973)
   Whose Mouse Are You? (1970)

Krementz, Jill
   Taryn Goes to the Dentist (1986)

Kumin, Maxine W.
   A Winter Friend (1961)

Lionni, Leo
  * *Frederick* (1967)
   Swimmy (1968)

Littledale, Freya
   The Magic Fish (1967)

Lyon, David
   The Runaway Duck (1985)

McCloskey, Robert
  * *Make Way for Ducklings* (1941)

McGovern, Ann
  * *Stone Soup* (1968)

McMillan, Bruce
   The Alphabet Symphony (1977)

Mosely, Keith
   Dinosaurs, A Lost World (1984)

Nodset, Joan L.
Who Took the Farmer's Hat? (1963)

Parker, Bertha Morris
The Wonders of the Seasons (1966)

Piper, Watty
* *The Little Engine That Could* (1961)

Radin, Ruth Yaffe
A Winter Place (1982)

Rey, H. A.
* *Curious George* (1941)
Other adventures of Curious George

Rey, Margaret and Alan J. Shalleck
Curious George at the Fire Station (1985)
More adventures of Curious George

Rockwell, Anne
Fire Engines (1986)

Rockwell, Harlow
My Dentist (1975)

Ross, Tony
Stone Soup (1987)

Rubel, Nicole
Bruno Brontosaurus (1983)

Sattler, Helen Roney
Train Whistles (1977)

Selsam, Millicent E.
Is This A Baby Dinosaur? (1971)

Sendak, Maurice
Chicken Soup With Rice (1962)

Seuss, Dr. (Theodore Geisel)
Green Eggs and Ham (1960)

Shaw, Charles
* *It Looked Like Spilt Milk* (1947, 1988)

Slater, Teddy
The Big Book of Real Fire Trucks and Fire Fighting (1987)

Slobodkina, Esphyr
* *Caps for Sale* (1940, 1987)

Steig, William
* *Doctor DeSoto* (1982)

Stinson, Kathy
Big or Little (1983)

Tafuri, Nancy
Have You Seen My Duckling? (1984)

Todd, Kathleen
Snow (1982)

Werner, Jane
The Fuzzy Duckling (1949)

Zallinger, Peter
Dinosaurs (1977)
Prehistoric Animals (1978)